EARLY YEARS OF TECH TITANS

Inspirational Stories for Children
About Innovators and Entrepreneurs

STELLA A. STARLING
Illustrated by Maria Savko
Chapters 2 & 7 illustrated by Julie Rabischung

THIS BOOK BELONGS TO

_____

DEDICATION

To my Moon and my Wings.

And to all the young dreamers and fearless explorers—this book is for you!

Learning can sometimes be tough, but like the amazing kids you'll read about here, you have a great spirit and endless curiosity that can brighten the world. Their stories show us that with hard work, we can accomplish impressive things.

Embrace your sense of wonder, dedicate yourself to hard work, and always believe with all your heart that anything is possible. So, keep dreaming big and reaching for the stars!

With all my love,

Mom

CONTENTS

INTRODUCTION

Hello, reader! Welcome to the exciting childhood world of our modern tech titans!

These individuals are referred to as tech titans because they have used technology to change the world, inventing smartphones, computers, laptops, solar cars, and software that enables the creation of self-driving cars, as well as websites that allow us to shop from home and so much more.

This book is all about incredible visionaries who, just like you, were once curious kids filled with wild ideas—and perhaps a love for chocolate ice cream, too! Some of them were nerds and brainiacs in their childhood, just like you, and they grew up to change the world. Yes, that iPhone you dream about was invented by one of the greatest tech giants of our time, who was also an artist. Can you guess who that might be?

In each chapter, you will meet amazing inventors and creators who leveraged their big dreams and hard work to transform how we live, play, and learn today. But don't worry; I won't bore you with stories of stiff CEOs and business jargon! Instead, we will dive into the childhood stories of these great innovators—because once upon a time, they were just kids with big dreams who sometimes faced many challenges, just like you.

I completely understand that being a kid can be tough at times, but it is also pretty fantastic! I bet you have some amazing stories of your own—quirky adventures, creative projects, or even the challenges you have overcome. So, get ready to explore how curiosity and imagination can lead to incredible things, just like in your own life!

Value the Advice of Mentors

It's important to have a mentor—someone you trust to ask for advice; even a good friend will do. Learning to accept help from good people is one lesson you will learn through some of the childhood stories in this book.

For example, a young boy named Larry Page grew up in a supportive family that emphasized academics and technology. This nurturing environment helped Larry develop his genius, ultimately leading him to co-found Google!

Never Give Up

Success doesn't happen instantly; sometimes, you have to keep trying and trying—just like when you were first learning to tie your shoelaces.

For example, a famous inventor named Jeff Bezos often faced failures rather than successes when he was young. Perhaps you tried making something, and it kept tumbling down, like a big bunch of Lego flowers or a boat that sails with a remote control. Jeff Bezos's story tells us that it's perfectly alright to fail; what's important is not giving up.

Do you know what Jeff Bezos famously invented? He invented Amazon, yes! That cool website your mom and everyone else uses to buy things.

Each failure Jeff faced turned into a lesson, teaching him persistence, which means it made him determined to keep trying. It's like building with Legos—your super-duper Lego house may get crushed when your dog runs over it or might fall and shatter into bits of colored blocks, but it's the rebuilding that matters.

Dream Big

Can you imagine a young Elon Musk, glued to his bedroom wall, which is covered with colorful rocket posters, dreaming of a world beyond the stars?

Do you know who Elon Musk is and what he invented?

The innovators you'll read about weren't born as geniuses; they were curious explorers like you.

They started with big dreams and ideas as kids. Perhaps you're already dreaming about new inventions, like creating self-tying shoelaces or even something as awesome as harnessing energy from lightning.

As you read these stories, enjoy the amusing mistakes that the innovators made as children, and let them motivate your own creativity, showing you that big dreams often stem from determination and some humorous outcomes.

I will introduce you to a little boy or girl you may have already heard of—or not; it doesn't matter. What's important is that you learn about their childhood and how they became some of the most significant figures of our time—oh, and also some of the wealthiest, driving cool cars and owning even cooler gadgets.

As we begin our journey through the lives of these young visionaries, let's celebrate the power of dreams and the remarkable potential within each child. Through their stories, may you find inspiration and recognize that every child holds the promise of greatness. So, what dreams will you ignite today?

Are you excited to get started? So am I! Turn the page, and let's begin with the rocket man himself.

CHAPTER
ONE
ELON MUSK:
BUILDING ROCKETS FROM
DREAMS TO REALITY

Let me introduce you to Elon Musk! You might know him as the amazing guy who creates rockets, satellites, and electric cars. But there's so much more to him!

Elon Musk is a super important inventor who loves coming up with new ideas. One of the coolest things he does is help make electric cars through his company, Tesla. Have you ever seen the Tesla Cybertruck on the road? It looks like something straight out of a sci-fi movie, doesn't it?

Electric cars are special because they don't run on regular gas, which means they're better for our planet, Earth. That makes Elon's work very important for a cleaner and greener future!

But that's not all! Elon also created SpaceX, a fascinating company that builds rockets to send people into space. Can you imagine living on Mars someday? That's one of his big dreams! He wants to make it possible for us to explore new worlds beyond our own—how cool is that?

In addition to rockets and cars, Elon Musk has even more exciting ideas. He's working on technology that could connect our brains to computers with tiny microchips, which could help us communicate in new ways. He's also thinking about building tunnels to make traveling faster and easier for everyone!

Elon Musk is like a real-life superhero for technology and space, always dreaming big and finding ways to make those dreams come true!

How the Rocket Man Got Started

Building rockets from dreams to reality sounds like a superhero path, right? But for Elon Musk, it was more of a "when-I-grow-up" kind of idea rather than a comic book fantasy. He was one determined kid who was not happy with just dreaming about great inventions.

While his friends were out playing soccer or collecting comic books, Elon was in his room, programming video games and messing around with any gizmo he could find. Yup, Elon enjoyed being in his bedroom, dreaming up wild ideas about space and other inventions.

So if any of you guys out there feel you are not a part of the team and are different, just remember it's alright to be who you are and enjoy doing what you like.

Elon didn't just dream about inventions; he managed to pull off some pretty good ones. For example, he invented and sold a game called Blastar for $500 at the ripe old age of 12 (Khan, n.d.).

Imagine trying to sell your homework instead of just handing it in. That's the kind of kid he was.

But it wasn't just about computers—oh no! You'd often find him unscrewing remote controls and taking apart gadgets, giving them a necessary checkup as if he were a doctor, and they were his patients. Tinkering wasn't just a hobby for him; it was a way to explore and understand how things worked, laying down the tracks for something bigger (Khan, n.d.).

Have you ever taken apart a gadget? The remote control of your kid sister's walking toy dog, maybe? Did the spring inside go pop, and you found you couldn't put it back together again?

Mistakes do happen when you have a curious mind, although it may not be good for your kid sister's toy. Exploring and wanting to know how things work is a good thing, so never stop asking questions.

Elon's childhood adventures didn't just stop at video games and tinkering. They shaped a whole lot of the person he became.

Ever heard of a saying that goes, "Fail harder and try better?"

FAIL HARDER
AND
TRY BETTER

Well, Elon lived by it because his inventions weren't always a success, but instead of sulking about the ones that didn't work, he'd tweak, test, and try again.

The Rocket Man as a Kid

Elon Musk was born on June 28, 1971, in Pretoria, South Africa. He spent most of his childhood in South Africa with his mother, brother, and sister. His mother was a huge mentor during his childhood.

A mentor is someone who helps you learn new things and grow. They are usually older and have lots of experience in something you want to get better at. A mentor supports you, gives you advice, and shares their knowledge so you can achieve your dreams! Do you have one?

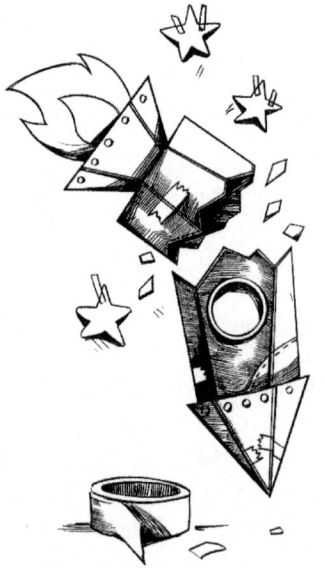

Elon's love for rockets didn't happen all at once. It started small, like when he built model rockets—sometimes they worked, and sometimes they didn't. Picture him launching a rocket and excitedly watching, hoping it will soar into the sky, but instead, it fizzles and falls, he would then go back to fix it until he finally hears the amazing whoosh as it soars into the sky.

These moments showed him how important it is to keep trying and learning from mistakes. When things got tough, instead of giving up, young Elon kept working hard—making changes, testing his ideas, and trying again (Alfar, 2024).

Well, the way I see it, kids, it's important to embrace failure, no matter how big or small they are; look at them as a learning opportunity. For Elon, each setback was merely new information, pushing him closer to success.

Elon Looked to Friends for Support

Maintaining friendships and a sense of belonging was important in helping Elon grow. Even though he's often seen as a lone genius, he loved learning with others because being among people who like the same things as us is fun. You find so much to talk about because you feel at ease in their company.

By joining local clubs, Elon met friends who were just as excited about technology and science as he was. It was in these groups that he discovered how valuable it is to work together to reach a shared goal (Editor BizNews, 2023).

These interactions weren't just about making friends; they were also about learning and growing. They gave him new ideas and inspired him to think even bigger. By being part of his local community, Elon formed friendships and also created a space where everyone could share what they knew, allowing all the members to grow and come up with new and exciting ideas together.

Have you ever thought about forming a "Brainiacs Club" or something else that helps you to get together with other pals your age and invent things?

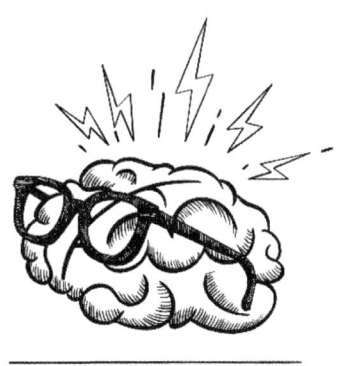

Maybe a cool game like Blastar. Or maybe to just have a space where you can talk about stuff that interests you uninterrupted with others just like you; stuff some kids would call nerdy but are fascinating subjects you all enjoy.

BRAINIACS CLUB

Early interests can lead to amazing successes later on. Just like Elon Musk, who went from coding a video game to launching a billion-dollar rocket, every interest matters.

Even simple things like playing with household gadgets and rockets can spark big ideas. So, keep your curiosity alive, and don't be afraid to ask questions or ask for help. Be around supportive friends who cheer on your dreams, and always remember that every expert started as a beginner!

The Bullying Incident

Musk has shared that he was bullied during his school years in South Africa. Until he was around 15 years of age and started fighting back by learning martial arts, Elon was bullied for being a bookworm and tech expert. Go figure, right?

The experience impacted him deeply and shaped his perspective on how he interacted with other people, while also making him determined to be successful. Elon didn't just give up and hide away in his room—he fought back (Piccotti & Carusso, 2022; Editor BizNews, 2023).

Elon Loved to Read

Imagine being a kid and diving into books filled with space adventures, laser beams, and robots. This was how Musk spent much of his childhood. His parents often thought he had a hearing problem because he was so lost in his world of books and tech that he rarely heard people talking to him.

I bet you've been asked if you are deaf a couple of times when you had your earbuds in and music on.

Sci-fi stories weren't just bedtime tales for Elon; they were seeds of ideas that would grow into something much bigger.

Okay, so perhaps reading Harry Potter won't make you a wizard with magical powers, but you will learn some cool words like "Wingardium Leviosa," which you can say under your breath hoping your chair will rise up and fly you right out of a boring lesson.

Books Opened New Dreams for Elon

When Musk read science fiction, it was like unlocking a door to endless possibilities. This kind of reading made him think beyond the ordinary. It's like when you finish a great book and start picturing yourself as a character in it, being part of the action, swinging lightsabers, or piloting spaceships.

Musk didn't just dream about these things; he began thinking about how he could make them real. He imagined technology that nobody had even thought possible yet. Sci-fi stretched his mind, teaching him to see the extraordinary in what others considered impossible. Like owning a company that built real rockets or inventing electric cars.

One of the most famous science fiction inspirations that stuck with Musk was the idea of traveling to Mars. Cool right?

We've all seen movies where humans live on Mars with cool gadgets and colorful domes. But for Musk, this wasn't just for the big screen— it was a goal. He saw sci-fi as a blueprint or master plan, showing how wild ideas can turn into groundbreaking projects. How many times has your Mom said, "Gosh you kids and your wild imagination!"

Books Elon Musk Loved as a Child (Sharma, 2024).

- Dune by Frank Herbert—A sci-fi novel about a faraway planet.
- The Hitchhikers Guide to the Galaxy by Douglas Adams—A sci-fi novel about a man who is sucked into space, moments before Earth is destroyed. Sounds interesting right?
- Foundation by Isaac Asimov—A book about the future and a mathematician who finds a way to predict the future.

Dreams to Reality

Well, did you know that Musk's dream of colonizing Mars isn't just a dream anymore; he's actively working on making it happen? It's an example of how science fiction can inspire real-world adventures.

These stories did more than just fuel his dreams; they taught him an important lesson: *If you can dream it, you can do it!*

It's like painting a picture—first, you imagine it, then you get your brushes and colors ready, and finally, you paint it into reality. This mindset motivated Musk to turn ambitious dreams into actual achievements. He believed that the limits were only as far as his imagination could stretch—and I guess he had a pretty big imagination.

Fictional worlds inspired real innovation, proving that today's imaginative stories can become tomorrow's inventions. Who knows? In time to come, we may have real-live Guardians of the Galaxy.

Musk's approach to life gives an important message to never shy away from dreaming big. Elon believes that big dreams help shape our future. Whether it's sending rockets into space or making cool electric cars, he believes that dreaming big helps us discover new things we never thought were possible. Dreaming is just the beginning. It's putting in the effort that turns those dreams into something fantastic!

His dreams challenge everyone else to pull up their socks and, as grown-ups say, "to think outside the box." And do not limit yourself to staying inside boundaries.

Do you have parents who make you push your limits or encourage you to dream big, even if you feel it's impossible? Then you are lucky, you have wise and understanding parents who believe you can reach the stars!

Be Happy to Be Different

Musk shows us that it's okay to be different, to strive for something others might laugh at because it's too "out there." Or weird.

After all, every remarkable invention started as someone's crazy idea. Creating a better world starts with imagining it first. For Musk, each rocket launch brings him one step closer to those visions, underlining the power of belief and hard work combined.

Science fiction has always sparked wild imaginations. For Musk, it ignited a fire that drove him toward groundbreaking innovations. He shows us that dramatic changes begin with something simple—a dream.

Never Give Up: Embrace Your Uniqueness!

Do you think Elon Musk's early love for space and technology, inspired by reading, helped him become one of the greatest tech leaders today?

Remember, if your paper airplane crashes more than it flies, that's okay! You're learning, just like Elon, a kid whose imagination soared higher than any kite.

Also, isn't it great that Elon enjoyed being a nerd and a bookworm? Unfortunately, we sometimes use mean names for people who are different or special—people who make our world better. Names like "nerd" or "bookworm" can be tough for some kids to hear. Elon was bullied for being different, but he didn't give up!

Our next chapter is about another special young kid who didn't have it easy, so put down that iPhone, and let's learn about its inventor.

Workbook Activity 1: What Are Your Dreams?

Use the blank pages after this chapter to write down or draw your dreams.

No matter how weird you may think they are, there could be something special in your ambitions. So, don't be afraid to be yourself and talk to your parents or friends about what you would like to do—build flying cars, take a trip around the world, learn 20 new languages, or even something less elaborate, like being a chef or a mechanic. Remember, your dreams make you special!

CHAPTER TWO

STEVE JOBS:
THE ARTISTIC VISIONARY

Steve Jobs is one of the greatest tech inventors of our time. He is one of the geniuses behind the invention of Apple products—yes, that iPhone you want for Christmas was partially invented by him.

Jobs wasn't just any tech guy; he was a bit like a magician with an artist's heart. Imagine someone who could take boring old computers and turn them into something as stylish as your favorite sneakers. Well, he didn't invent sneakers, but he did have a hand in designing that cool-looking MacBook you wish you owned and the sleek iPad you often use.

Steve's journey into tech greatness started, like many superhero origin stories—in a garage. Yep, young Steve spent hours in his family's California garage, not fighting crime but taking apart gadgets just to see how they ticked. Kind of like Tony Stark.

It wasn't all hard work and no play, though, for Steve, who lived a colorful life as a kid. He had a rebellious streak that made school something of a rollercoaster ride for him, meaning he had ups and downs. You see, Steve wasn't too keen on traditional schooling; instead, he let his curiosity and a hint of mischief guide his learning adventures. Are you going: "Aha, that's who I want to be. A cool kid who knows what he wants." Well, perhaps. Let's explore more of Steve's childhood.

In this chapter. We'll dive into the world of Steve Jobs as a kid, a time when he learned to combine his love for technology with the arts in awesome ways that changed the way people look at computer and smartphone designs.

Steve was a special kind of tech kid; he would be tinkering, pulling apart, and reconnecting gadgets in the garage while becoming mesmerized by the beauty of calligraphy at college.

Do you know what *Calligraphy* is?

Calligraphy is a special way of writing that makes letters look like art!

You can use a pen or brush to write your name or to draw letters in a fancy, artistic sort of way. Calligraphers are people who write in calligraphy and create swirly, decorative letters that can make anything from cards to invitations look special. It's like turning words into a pretty picture! Go on, hit your computer, and search for some images of calligraphy, and you will understand how special Steve Jobs was; he had a vision, and that was to blend art and technology.

Steve Jobs' Early Interests

Steve Jobs's story begins in Mountain View, California, where he lived with his parents, Paul and Clara Jobs; they adopted Steve when he was a baby (Piccotti, 2023).

Even though Steve knew he was adopted, his relationship with his adoptive parents was very special. They believed in him, and that made a huge difference in his life. While he faced some challenges growing up—like feeling a bit different from his classmates—he always had a strong support system at home.

Later in life, Steve found out more about his biological parents and learned that his biological father was from Syria, while his mother was from Switzerland (Piccotti, 2023). But throughout his childhood, it was Paul and Clara who shaped him into the brilliant and innovative person he became. They taught him valuable lessons about hard work, creativity, and following his dreams—all things that helped him change the world with Apple!

They were great parents who encouraged Steve's curious nature, even when he kept taking apart gadgets that worked just fine. What would your parents say if you took apart the TV remote? Let's not find out!

Steve's Father Was His Mentor

Paul Jobs was the first person to inspire Steve's curiosity to take things apart and fix them; You see, Paul was a fixer-upper type of person himself; he was a mechanic who would buy and fix up old cars to resell them for more money than he spent buying and fixing them up. Cool, right?

So, Paul taught Steve about the value of craftsmanship and how to get cheap parts that could be fixed up and reused, which, by the way, was part of how Steve and his partner managed to invent the first Apple computer—they used bits and pieces of second-hand tech (*Paul Jobs*, n.d.).

The family garage became a playground of sorts, where young Steve learned the art of building and repairing gadgets. Steve spent hours taking apart and putting together electronic gadgets so that he became pretty good at repairing stuff and I guess he may have even invented a few cool gadgets with them. These experiences not only helped build Steve's mechanical skills but also made him confident and hungry to succeed.

Do You Have a Special Space?

Do you have a space like this where you can explore and learn about how things work, a special place to indulge in your favorite hobby? If you don't, and you would like one, why not talk to your parents or caregiver about setting up your special space? Even a section in your room could become your personal garage.

School Was Not Easy For Steve

Despite his growing interest in technology, Steve struggled at school but not because he was bad at studies; he found standard schooling boring and was not interested in all of the subjects he had to learn. Do you agree? Are there some subjects you absolutely love and others that make you go, *yawn*!?

Steve was no dumbo; he did not like *standard* learning because he had his pet subjects.

Do you know what they were?

Mathematics and electronics stood out as his favorites, and Steve pursued those subjects with interest until he evolved into a genius who could combine his creativity with his love for maths and tech. Awesome right?

He didn't like just following rules all the time. Instead, Steve loved exploring and learning about things that made him curious. This helped him become really good at things in his own special way, thinking differently from other kids.

Perhaps you love history and enjoy learning about ancient civilizations, but you dislike math and feel bored working with numbers. Each kid has his or her unique strengths, and those must be cultivated.

Steve Jobs, the Prankster

In middle and high school, Steve was known as a prankster. He was considered a rebel because he had a free spirit and disliked standard education. He enjoyed playing innocent pranks on his friends and maybe even his teachers, but it all shows that Steve wasn't just stuck in his own world—he enjoyed a good laugh and making others laugh too.

Who is the class clown in your school? The kid who brings a frog to school or makes goofy faces when the teacher is not looking?

School Helped Steve

Steve greatly appreciated school and benefited from going because it was in school that he discovered subjects that truly captivated him and also found his friend and future business partner. So, you see why your parents or caregivers insist on a good education; school opens up new paths for us to explore and decide who we want to be.

Steve's Dropout From College

After briefly attending Reed College in Portland, Oregon, at 17 years of age, Steve dropped out after just one semester. There are several reasons listed for this decision, such as Steve wanting to pursue only specific studies that interested him and would assist him in his future endeavors. He was also dealing with financial problems as his parents could not afford to fund his college expenses. So although he highly valued the benefit of education, Steve decided to drop out and pursue only targeted subjects in a bid to continue his learning and reduce the financial strain on his parents.

Despite not completing his formal education, he continued to check out classes that interested him, such as calligraphy, which later influenced Apple product designs and is why they look sleeker and nicer than other smartphones or laptops—they were designed by a tech whiz with an artist's heart.

About dropping out, Steve says it was a very scary decision, but he knew what he wanted and pursued those subjects. Dropping out of college was not easy for Steve; he had no dorm and would sleep on the floor of friends' dorm rooms, and since money was scarce, he would collect and return empty Coke bottles for the deposit, which he used to buy food (Haroon, 2020).

Tough, right? But through it all, he did manage to get an education that helped him become one of the greatest tech giants of all time.

So you see, dropping out of college and pursuing a dream is no piece of cake; it's a decision Steve made out of necessity, but he was passionate and had a goal. With goals and lots of hard work, you can achieve dreams.

What does this tell us?

It says that obstacles should not get in the way of achieving your dreams. And not being good at everything does not mean you are a failure; it means you have to find your special ability—like a spidey sense. You may not be a math genius or an artist, but you will have something that makes you special. Sports perhaps? Dancing or chess? You may know or not, but do go ahead and explore and embrace your special qualities, no matter how big or small they are.

Steve's Friendship With Steve Wozniak:

In high school, Steve Jobs made an awesome friend named Steve Wozniak, and guess what? They were both total tech geniuses! How wild is it to find someone with the same name as you who also loves tinkering with computers? It's like they were destined to be pals!

Can you picture their first meeting? It probably went something like this:

I mean, how hilarious is that? Two Steves bonding over lunch and their love for tech!

So, it wasn't just about sharing names; these two boys discovered they were super into electronics and computers. They spent tons of time hanging out, working on fun projects together, and getting into all kinds of techy adventures. Whether they were building weird gadgets or figuring out how to make cool things work, their friendship was filled with laughter and discovery.

They played off each other's ideas, bouncing thoughts back and forth like a game of ping pong. One Steve would say, "What if we tried this?" and the other would reply, "Yeah, let's make it happen!" Their friendship was like a creative playground where they could turn wild ideas into reality.

So, not only did they share a name, but they also shared a passion that led to some fantastic inventions! Together, they learned that having a buddy who gets your interests can make creating, experimenting, and having fun even more exciting. Friendship truly is a powerful thing, especially when you're both on the same techy wavelength!

The Blue Box

The two friends invented a device they called the "blue box," which allowed them to make free long-distance phone calls. This was at a time before smartphones and WhatsApp or FaceTime were there to call anyone anywhere in the world.

At that time, phones were landlines connected to wires, so you couldn't just leave the house with them. They had rotating diallers; you may have seen them at your grandparent's house—round disks with holes and numbers in them, you used to dial a number.

People had to call their network operator and connect through them when they wanted to make a long-distance phone call—like calling someone in another state or even another country. Long-distance calls were very expensive, and people rarely made them.

The two friends created the blue box device, which they used to hack into telephone networks, tricking the systems that allowed them to connect to phones far away instead of going through the operator. So they could make long-distance phone calls for free (Yazdinian, 2024).

Jobs and Wozniak were very successful because they were interested in the same things. They later became business partners, and together, they founded the Apple company—guess where the company was first based? In Steve Jobs's family garage, of course! (*Steve Jobs*, 2023).

Dreams Are Important

Hey kids, as we explored the exciting and also tough life of Steve Jobs in his early years, we discovered how mixing creativity and curiosity turned his mind into a super cool science lab full of awesome ideas!

Can you believe that playing with electronics in a garage and doodling funky letters in the name of calligraphy could kickstart a whole revolution of beautifully designed tech gadgets?

It's like discovering your LEGO blocks can turn into a spaceship's control panel! Well, maybe not, but Steve's story shows us that mixing art and tech is like adding sprinkles to a cupcake—it's magical!

Young Steve was never shy to think outside the box—or the garage, so to speak!—which helped him to dream big and think out of the ordinary.

Steve's story is a reminder that exploring interests, even ones that seem unrelated to what is expected of you, can create surprising connections. Therefore, if you find yourself daydreaming about robots while reading a comic book, you may be onto something significant!

Parents remember that encouraging exploration and allowing kids to nurture their whims can help cultivate future trailblazers. Just like Steve absorbed bits of knowledge from everywhere, learning becomes an adventure, showing us that sometimes, innovation starts with a simple question: What if?

Our next inventor is someone who developed something you all use or will do so in the future. Have you heard of Canva?

Workbook Activity 2: Creating Fun Calligraphy Art

Do you want to try your hand at calligraphy? It's loads of fun, so here are some ideas for you to use calligraphy creatively. You can use the provided blank pages to get started.

Step 1: Go online and type in the following search terms: "Simple Calligraphy Tutorials for Kids." Or "Practicing Calligraphy for Kids." Using these search terms, you will find plenty of videos that will help you get started.

Step 2: Do a few fun practice rounds. Use a blank page after this chapter for your first practice.

Step 3: Choose a creative project to use your super-new talent. Here are a few ideas to help you get started.

Birthday Card Creation: Design a personalized birthday card for a friend or family member with calligraphy writing. You can decorate the card with drawings or stickers to make it extra special.

Inspirational Quote Poster: Choose their favorite quote or saying from your favorite superhero and create a colorful poster. Use calligraphy to write the quote in big, bold letters and decorate the poster with illustrations and stickers.

Here's an example:

Creativity is intelligence having fun. –Albert Einstein

- **Thank You Notes:** Write a thank you note for gifts or acts of kindness you received. For a Nana who baked your favorite cookies or a friend who helped you with your homework—it will be just as good as a hug.

- **Alphabet Art:** Create an artistic representation of the alphabet. You can write each letter in calligraphy style and then decorate each letter with drawings, patterns, or colors that correspond to items that start with that letter. For example, A for apple, B for balloon.

- **Friendship Scrolls:** Get together with your friends and make friendship scrolls for each other. You can each write a positive message or a fun memory you share with your friend using calligraphy. You can roll it up and tie it with a ribbon for a lovely keepsake.

Calligraphy

Calligraphy

Calligraphy

Calligraphy

CHAPTER
THREE
MELANIE PERKINS:
DESIGNS CANVA

Have you ever designed a birthday card for your mom using computer graphics?

Computer graphics and designing are super easy now, thanks to an awesome lady named Melanie Perkins and her brainchild, Canva!

With it, we can create videos, design fab postcards, birthday invitations, social media graphics, presentations, and a whole lot of other creative graphics quite easily.

Have you used Canva before? It's very popular among school kids who use it for all sorts of projects. Like class presentations, and so on. In this chapter, we will learn about Melanie's childhood habits and dreams that led to her inventing Canva and becoming one of the richest people in the world today.

Also watch out for the exciting workbook at the end of this chapter, one that will help you to check out how good you can be with Canva.

Who Is Melanie Perkins?

She's the creative mastermind behind Canva, a graphic designing platform that lets anyone become a design wizard by using tools to create magical illustrations with just a few clicks.

Born in the sunny city of Perth, Australia, Melanie was surrounded by inspiration. Imagine a little girl running around with a paintbrush in one hand and a toolbox in the other—yep, that's Melanie! Her home was a cheerful mix of paints, engineering toys, and endless giggles, where creativity flowed like a never-ending fountain of ideas.

With a teacher mom who could paint a sunset from memory and an engineer dad who could fix anything with a twist here and a turn there, it's no wonder Melanie's interests were as varied as they come (Winford, 2024).

Growing up, she found herself surrounded by ideas and experiments. However, Melanie once wanted to be a figure skater and dedicated a portion of her childhood toward this passion; she would wake up at 4.30 a.m. to head out for practice, but life had other plans for Melanie, and she did not pursue her dream of becoming a professional skater (Admin, 2022).

It's okay to experiment and change your interests until you find something that takes hold of you. It may take several years for some of you to discover those interests, while others may already know what they want to do or be as adults.

Melanie, a Teen Entrepreneur

Have you ever wanted to earn some extra pocket money and set up a lemonade stand? Or bake cookies to sell, or perhaps offer to bathe the dog, or even do your friend's homework—for a fee? Shh... let's not talk about that.

Well, Melanie didn't just sell food or drinks at just 14 years of age; she embarked on her first entrepreneurial venture by selling handmade silk-screen blankets.

What are handmade silk-screen blankets, you wonder? Well, silk-screening is something like stenciling, where a mesh is used to transfer a print onto fabric. This is what Melanie did to create artsy blankets, which she sold (Admin, 2022).

This experience was super important for her! It taught her all about how to run a business, make people want to buy things, and how to talk with customers. Selling blankets wasn't just about collecting money to buy stuff; it was like a fun workshop where she learned how to make her products look cool and keep track of her earnings. By doing this, Melanie discovered how exciting and tricky running a business could be, which made her want to learn even more about being an entrepreneur! (Admin, 2022).

I bet Melanie didn't run off and spend her hard-earned money on the latest video game or sweets; she probably saved up for her next big project.

Oh, and by the way, Melanie and her husband are listed among the richest people in Australia—yes, she is a billionaire (Karmali, N, 2024).

Who Is an Entrepreneur?

An entrepreneur is like a superhero in the business world! They come up with cool ideas for new products or services, just like inventors. Then, they work really hard to make those ideas happen. Entrepreneurs are the ones who start their own businesses, like a lemonade stand or a toy store. They take risks, which means they try things that might be a little scary, like putting all your saved pocket money into baking cookies you hope to sell. Well, entrepreneurs take risks for the chance to create something amazing and share it with everyone!

If you have a great idea and want to turn it into something real, you could be an entrepreneur too!

Melanie Was a Go-Getter in School

In addition to her creative pursuits, Melanie was involved in a lot of business-type projects in school. She was a girl with a target, and this may have driven her to seek more knowledge and experience on how to become a good entrepreneur.

Melanie Loved Joining in Various Activities

In school, Melanie got super involved in fun business programs and competitions that helped her become a business whiz! She jumped into all sorts of activities where she could practice her love for business and learn awesome new skills. These programs were like treasure chests filled with cool lessons about planning, teamwork, and coming up with fresh ideas. Plus, competing made her tougher, like a superhero training for a big battle!

Melanie Embraced Team Work

By joining these programs, Melanie didn't just learn a bunch of stuff; she also met other kids who loved business as much as she did! They became her pals and helped her get even more excited about being an entrepreneur. This whole adventure let her practice being a leader and working together with others, setting her up for future success when she started her own company with her two partners! Can you see how finding a bunch or even one friend who shares similar interests to yours can be empowering and loads of fun?

The Birth of Canva and Melanie's Vision

As a university student, Melanie Perkins had a big idea that would one day change the way people think about design.

Melanie imagined a world where people didn't have to be super-talented artists or spend a long time learning tricky computer programs to master graphic design to make beautiful videos or pictures. She saw how hard it was for kids to use difficult graphic design tools. Some can be very complicated and frustrating to use, right?—because not all of us are computer whizzes?

So, Melanie realized that there was a need for an easy and friendly online tool that anyone could use, no matter how bad they were at art or navigating computer programs.

One that even your grandpa or grandma can use to make cool Christmas cards or those embarrassing family videos of a time when you were four years old and your front teeth had all fallen out, and you were grinning like Gramps without his dentures.

Melanie was inspired by these challenges to create something new and exciting. She would have thought, *What if everyone had the power to design without needing special skills?*

This question led her to create Canva—a computer program with tools that would make design easy for everyone. But this wasn't just a one-person effort. Melanie teamed up with two other people, Cliff Obrecht and Cameron Adams, and together they co-founded Canva. As a team, they set out on a mission to make design accessible to all people (Danielson, 2025).

Canva Grew Because Melanie Listened to What People Wanted

Building something as remarkable as Canva wasn't just about having a brilliant idea. It required teamwork and a willingness to listen and learn from others.

Melanie knew that collaboration would be the key to success. So, she gathered feedback from friends, peers, and early users of Canva. They tried out the tool and shared what they loved and what could be improved. Melanie took this input seriously and used it to refine Canva, ensuring it met the needs of its users.

You see, kids, how smart Melanie was? She had several positive traits that benefited her:

- She was willing to work as a team.
- She accepted help from others
- She asked for feedback and didn't get all huffy at the reviews; she took the good and bad stuff people said about Canva to make it even better.

In the end, she and her partners had a winning program, all because they accepted help, worked together, and were humble enough to learn from what other people were saying about their invention.

Working together and helping each other with useful feedback became super important for Canva's growth.

Melanie's adventurous and creative way of thinking reminds us all that when we see a problem; we can choose to tackle it instead of running away. Just like when she looked at complicated design tools and decided to make them easier for everyone. She made designing fun and easy, inspiring many others to think of creative ways to solve real-life problems.

Believe in Your Potential

Do you agree that everyone must believe in their potential?

If you have parents, caregivers, or teachers who instill confidence in you, it will be easier for you to achieve great things, just like Melanie turned her entrepreneurial skills and graphic designing talents into a successful design platform. Every kid has the potential to someday make a big impact on the world!

Melanie's proactive involvement in both creative and business endeavors set her apart. Her ability to balance these interests demonstrated a maturity and foresight that hinted at her potential to transform simple ideas into impactful projects. The adults in her life did not shut her down; rather, they encouraged her entrepreneurial behavior—understanding that she was more advanced in her thinking than most teens of her time.

Finally, it was a combination of support, creativity, business acumen, and determination that propelled her forward, making her well-prepared to face the business world, which she did in a big way!

Workbook Activity 3: Canva Vision Board

Okay kids, here's the most exciting part of this chapter, your special project.

Using the free Canva tool, create a digital vision board that will highlight your goals using images, colors, and inspirational quotes. You can add a collage of images representing people who inspire you to reach your goals, paired with a short description of why they motivate you.

A digital vision board on Canva is like a super cool online poster where you can collect and organize pictures, words, and ideas that represent your dreams and goals! Instead of using scissors and glue like a regular vision board, you use a computer or tablet to find images and designs that inspire you. You can choose templates and add everything you love, like photos of places you want to visit, things you want to learn, or what you want to be when you grow up. It can be one template or several, so you can separate your visions and goals into different sections.

It's a fun and creative way to see your dreams all in one place, and you can change it whenever you want! When you look at your vision board, it will remind you of your dreams and help you believe you can achieve them!

Step 1—Create an Outline: This will be a draft of what your vision board will contain. If it's going to be more than one template/section, decide on a topic for each and what you want to add there. Be precise with exactly what you want to add to each section; that way, you know what material to gather before you start the project.

Step 2—Refer to Your Outline: Choose what to include in each template of your vision board. Collect your pictures, quotes, and other material you want to include in it. If you don't have digital images of everything you want to add, you will have to scan and add them to your picture gallery.

Step 3—Search for "Canva Free Online Vision Board Maker:" Open the app and explore the features and suggestions listed there. You will see examples and videos on how to use Canva, which makes the entire process super easy.

Step 4—Look for Additional Help: If you need more help using Canva, use these search terms to find a video tutorial that will make using Canva easier. "How to create a vision board in Canva."

Happy creating, kids!

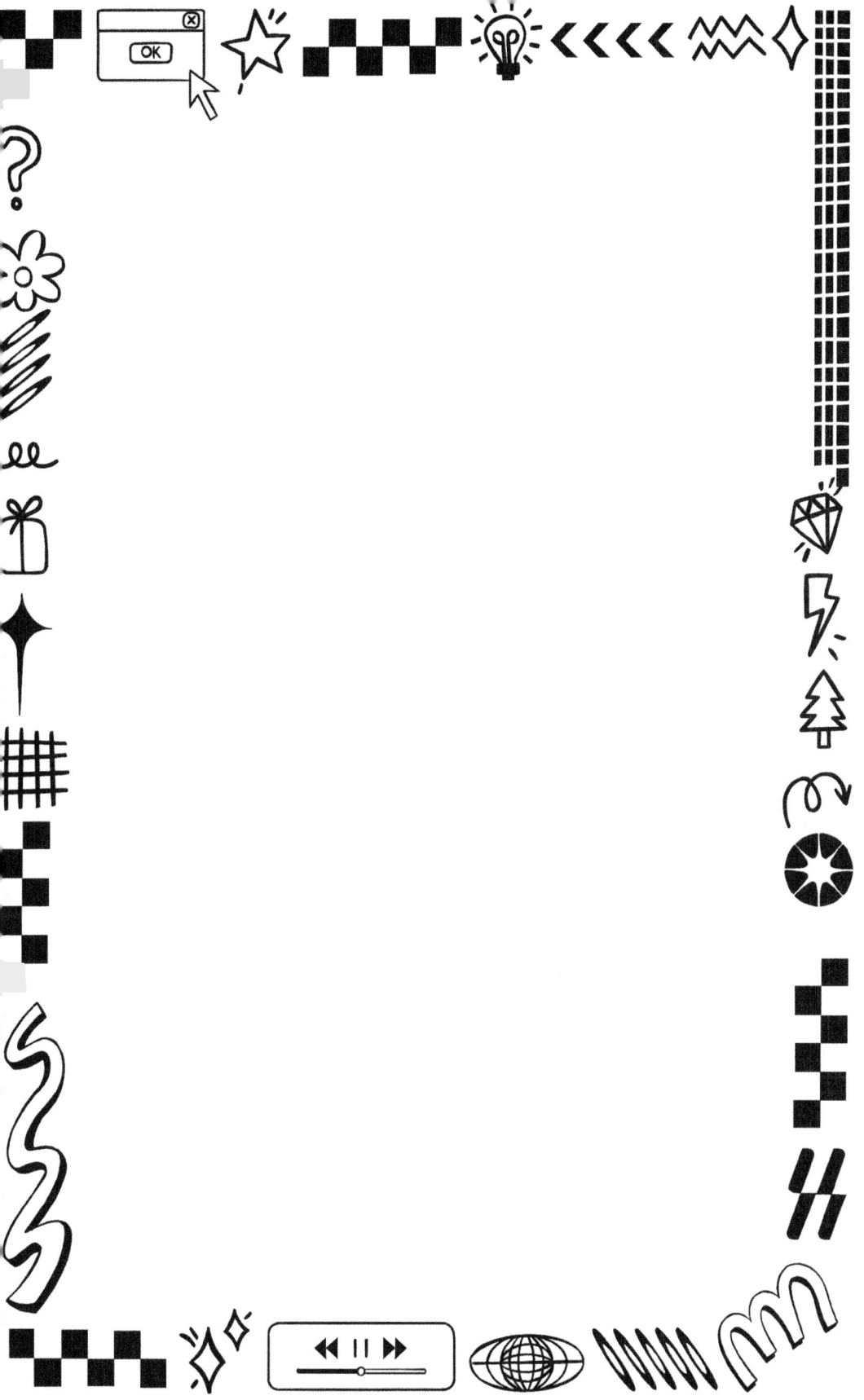

CHAPTER FOUR

MARK ZUCKERBERG:
THE SHY KID WHO INVENTED FACEBOOK

Are you a shy kid who stresses over meeting new kids, going to parties, or being out of your home—your comfort zone?

Do you dread social events where you have to make small talk?

Our next tech giant will show you that being a shy kid or even getting labeled as an introvert by no means stops you from achieving great things.

An introvert is a person who likes to spend time alone or with just a few close friends instead of being in big groups. They often feel happy and recharged when they read a book, do puzzles, or play quietly. It's like when you enjoy playing on your own sometimes, and that's perfectly okay! Introverts are just a little different in how they like to enjoy their time. They can be great listeners and think deeply about things. They also make great friends and can be very understanding.

Here's a fun fact: Lots of geniuses we know are introverts (Fabritius, 2023). So go ahead and embrace who you are but never let it hold you back.

Say hello to Mark Zuckerberg, often recognized as an introverted genius. He's the guy who invented Facebook, setting the benchmark for other popular social media platforms we use today.

Yes, that's right. Even if you don't have a Facebook account yet, it's one of the world's most popular social media platforms that many believe also inspired ones you like, such as Instagram, TikTok, and Pinterest.

Mark Zuckerberg as a Kid

Mark Zuckerberg was born in White Plains, New York, and from an early age, he showed a remarkable talent for computer programming.

The Invention of ZuckNet

At just 12 years old, Mark created his first software program called "ZuckNet."

ZuckNet was a messaging application—a chat app that allowed people to communicate through computers—kind of like WhatsApp or Messenger.

Mark's father, Edward Zuckerberg, was a dentist and would often need to communicate with his dental staff at the office, but he needed a way to talk to them without having to shout across rooms.

Imagine Mark's father shouting out to his staff:

Mr. Plod would be out of there like a shot!

So considering this need for discreet communication, Mark, who was not yet a teen, used his genius to invent ZuckNet. It was a genius app that allowed his father to send messages to his staff, quietly, through his computer and, at the same time, allowed the Zuckerberg family to communicate with each other because the dental office was a part of their home (Wagner, 2017).

Mark's dad could send his staff and kids messages from his office without having to shout, "Hey, kids, let's go out for ice cream as soon as I finish pulling out Mr. Plod's teeth!"

Mark Was Encouraged to Be a Genius

Do you have parents, a grandparent, a teacher, an older sibling, a best friend, or anyone else who is always encouraging you to reach your full potential?

They are people who can see you are special and want to direct you on a path to success. Not everyone has someone watching over them, and that's okay too, because you can still decide on the path you want to take by accepting your strengths and weaknesses and working to improve both.

Growing up in an environment that encouraged him to explore and be creative played a significant role in shaping Zuckerberg's future. His mother, Karen, was a psychiatrist, and his father, although a dentist, also had a deep interest in technology.

Mark's parents recognized their son's potential early on. They supported his growing curiosity by hiring a private tutor called David Newman. Newman worked with Mark once a week and said it was challenging to stay ahead of young Zuckerberg's ever-expanding knowledge in computing (Biography, 2019). Wow, imagine being smarter than your teacher.

Mark the Shy Genius

Mark was never short of inspiration, probably because his father too was interested in tech, and he was given a lot of support by his parents.

He spent his childhood crafting computer games with his friends, most of whom were artists. Mark would invite them over, and together, they would create characters and stories—like comics—that he would then use to create video games. Can you imagine a bunch of friends all into gaming, with vivid imaginations, creating awesome characters they could then turn into players in their video games?

What an awesome friend Mark would have been.

Would you like to have a friend who can create video games from characters you invented? If you did, what type of character would you invent?

Mark Valued Feedback

Mark's love for programming, combined with the group projects he and his friends engaged in, led him to excel in both creativity and technical skills.

Building the games with input from his friends helped Mark to understand the importance of user engagement, which means the person using the computer program gets involved with the creator by giving feedback.

Kind of like when you give your feedback to your mom on the Brussels sprouts she cooked for dinner as opposed to the pizza you were hoping to get.

Working with user feedback was something that helped Mark a lot when he later developed Facebook, which is based a lot on user preferences.

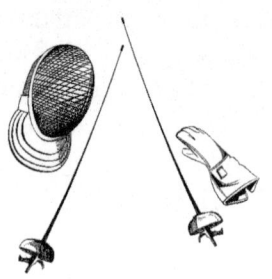

Mark's High School Life

Zuckerberg attended Phillips Exeter Academy, where he was a whiz at studies and also became the captain of the fencing team. Not bad for a shy computer kid, right?

Mark Invents the Music App in College

During his time in high school, Mark continued to explore and feed his love for technology. So, for his senior project, he developed a music player app he named Synapse; it was an early version of what you may recognize today as platforms like Spotify, Pandora, or Apple Music.

Synapse would study the user's music preferences and then recommend songs, albums, and artists for them to explore. It was a pretty amazing invention at that time, and companies such as AOL and Microsoft took notice by offering to buy Synapse and also hire Mark to work for them before he even graduated. However, Mark declined their offers, signaling his desire to create something even bigger (Van, 2016).

University and More Awesome Inventions

After graduating, Mark went on to Harvard University. He was already quite famous by then for his computer programming genius.

At Harvard, he studied both psychology and computer science, which says you can mix and match different subjects. Remember how calligraphy helped Steve Jobs with his Apple designs?

Well, Mark was already an established computer genius and by studying psychology, he explored a unique blend of subjects. One helped him to understand human behavior, while the other armed him with the technical skills necessary for innovative digital solutions.

The Invention of CourseMatch

Mark soon became known as the go-to developer on campus due to his previous successes and ongoing projects. During his sophomore year, he created CourseMatch, a program that helped students choose courses each semester based on what their peers selected. This helped them to choose popular classes and also analyze trends followed by the previous batches (Van, 2016).

The Invention of FaceMash

Another platform Mark created while at Harvard was FaceMash. This guy was on a roll, right?

Mark said he created FaceMash as a fun project; it was available to students of Harvard and presented them with two pictures, most of the time of a boy and a girl, out of which the students were asked to choose the better-looking person (Van, 2016). Kind of like a vote to decide who was more popular.

Can you imagine how controversial FaceMash would have been, with students clamoring to know if they got more votes than the other person?

FaceMash became so popular that Harvard authorities had to switch off their internet system to stop students from using the app because some of them were offended and angry at being included in FaceMash. There were several complaints from students who said

Mark used their pictures without their permission. Mark did get into trouble over this and had to publicly apologize (Van, 2016).

Imagine if you were to paste pictures of boys and girls in your school on all the lockers and then ask everyone to vote for the best looking; what a big ruckus there would be? You most likely will get called to the principal's office.

Also, don't you think FaceMash would have given Mark ideas for developing Facebook?

Mark Zuckerberg's early years show how important support, along with determination and curiosity, can lead to great success. These experiences prepared him for his influential work at Harvard, where he started to create social networking. By constantly exploring and learning, Mark showed how a mix of creative thinking, personal interests, and education can lead to valuable contributions in technology.

The Birth of Facebook

Facebook was launched at Harvard University by Mark Zuckerberg and his fellow students. Originally it was named "TheFacebook;" the platform was designed for Harvard students to connect and engage with each other online; over time the name changed and simply became Facebook (Hall, 2024).

Aren't you glad the name changed to just Facebook dropping the "The." Imagine people saying, "I am on The Facebook." Or "Have you checked The Facebook!"

In case you are not familiar with Facebook and are more of an Instagram or TikTok fan, Facebook works by allowing people to make their own special profiles with their personal details; it's a platform where for example, they can tell the world about their favorite ice cream flavors, chat with friends, share photos of places they have been to, and interact in a big digital playground!

At first, The Facebook, was only for Harvard students, but then it grew in popularity like a snowball rolling down a hill, as kids from other cool schools like Yale and Stanford joined the platform. Before long, Facebook became the most popular place for students to hang out online, kind of like the coolest treehouse that everyone wanted to join!

It was also the perfect kind of place for shy kids to socialize and get to know people without leaving the comfort of their home or dorm rooms.

Facebook Becomes a Giant Success—Mark Drops Out of Harvard

As more and more kids started joining Facebook, Zuckerberg saw it turning into a super big deal, like finding a never-ending stash of cookies! Score!

He had a lightbulb moment and thought, "Wow, this could be HUGE!" So, he made a big decision—he packed up his books and decided to drop out of Harvard, kind of like jumping off a diving board to focus on making Facebook the coolest place ever! This brave leap helped Mark to turn Facebook from a small college club into a giant, worldwide playground where everyone could share cat videos and funny memes.

By putting all his time and energy into Facebook, Zuckerberg proved he was ready to take social networking to the next level—like becoming the superhero of online fun (Hall, 2024).

Keep in mind, kids, that Mark dropped out of Harvard after achieving quite a lot in terms of education. He was well established as a tech whiz, had several successful apps under his belt, and had studied computer science and psychology, although he did not complete the degrees.

Let's not forget that he was already approached by big companies like AOL and Microsoft for his Synapse app, so he knew with Facebook he had a mega win, and taking the chance to leave university and develop Facebook was a lucrative move. It was not a last-minute decision or one that was made with no thought to his future. Mark knew he had a winner with Facebook.

Shy Kids Can Be Trailblazers

So do you agree that even though Mark Zuckerberg was known for being a bit shy and reserved, he turned into an amazing trailblazer in tech, always coming up with cool ideas, making friends with people who liked the same things, and proving that you can shine bright no matter how quiet you start out!

It's not always the bold, talkative kids that do special things; take your time, accept yourself for who you are, and don't let anything hold you back.

Have you asked your mom or dad to order you anything from Amazon recently? Yes? Well, our next tech giant made that possible. Let's turn to the next chapter.

Workbook Activity 4: Mission Facebook Exploration & Usage Log

Should you choose to accept this mission, you must make sure to complete it. Choose your team carefully and keep track of your research subjects, aka your parents, grandparents, or any other adult using Facebook.

Objective: Analyze why adults enjoy using Facebook and track their daily usage.

Materials Needed:

- Access to a computer or tablet with Facebook (with parent permission)

- Notebooks or printable worksheets

- Pens or pencils

- Timer or watch—to sneakily track usage! Shh...

Step 1—Research and Discussion:

Have a group discussion about Facebook with your friends. Ask them what they think adults like about the app, for example, staying connected with friends, sharing updates, joining groups, and so on. Write down their ideas on the blank pages provided after this chapter.

Step 2—Surveys: Create a simple survey for you and your friends to conduct with adults using Facebook: Parents, family members, or teachers—like the cool ones who mind helping you out!

The survey can include questions like these:

- What do you enjoy most about using Facebook?

- How often do you use Facebook in a day?

- What features do you use the most: Sharing photos, messaging, news feeds, or any other?

Make sure to ask them politely and in a non-intrusive manner:

Step 3—Usage Log: Ask each of your friends running the survey to create a Facebook account (with permission) and observe how long they use the app for one week. They should note the time they log in and log out each day. If your parents are against this step, you can scrap it—it's no big deal.

Step 4—Analysis: After a week, get together with your friends and review your logs.

You can analyze the following based on the answers you got from the adults you surveyed and from the kids who were able to create Facebook accounts:

- How much time did they spend on Facebook?

- What activities did they engage in while logged in?

- Did their usage change over the days? If so, what might have caused that?

Step 5—Presentation: Finally, get together and present your findings on:

- The reasons adults like Facebook are based on your surveys.

- Your friends' usage patterns as well as their thoughts on how social media affects their lives.

This activity will teach you about critical thinking in terms of social media and will help you to understand different perspectives on why some platforms are more appealing.

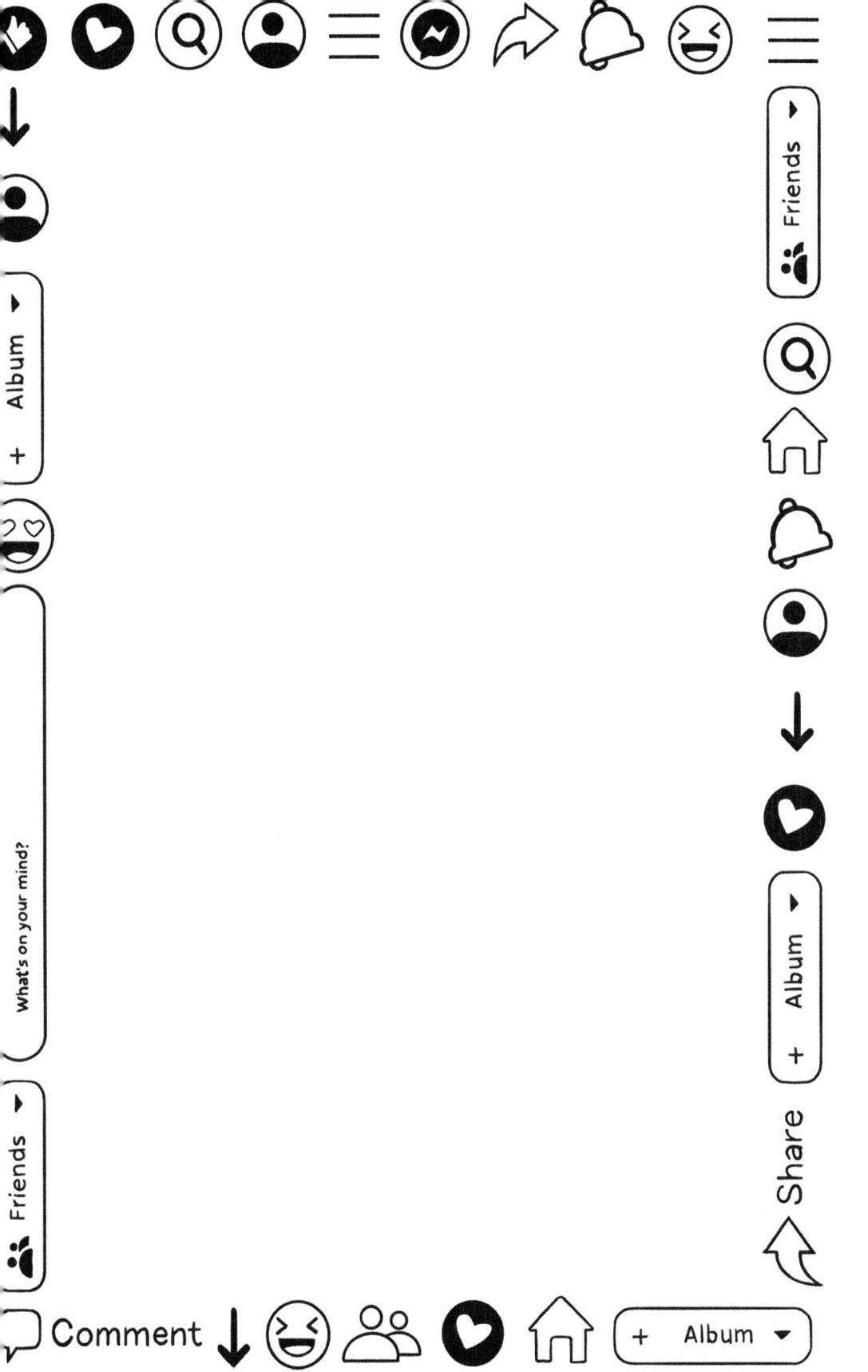

CHAPTER FIVE
JEFF BEZOS:
FROM GARAGE TO GLOBAL MARKETPLACE

Do you often get packages delivered to your home from a place called Amazon, with a type of smiley arrow at the bottom of the word "Amazon?" I bet your household does, and perhaps you have ordered a bunch of stuff from there yourself.

Jeff Bezos is the founder of Amazon, which is the world's biggest online store where people can buy almost anything they want with a few clicks on their computer. Jeff is a successful entrepreneur just like Melanie Perkins, but he had a very different childhood.

Jeff Bezos' remarkable exploits from a garage in Albuquerque, New Mexico, to creating a global marketplace is quite the story. Imagine a young boy, screwdriver in hand, eyes gleaming with the wonderment of discovery as he dismantles gadgets just to understand how they tick.

What's up with these tech-whiz kids dismantling electronic gadgets, right? Well, it's called curiosity and the need to know. I bet there are several gadgets in your home that you would like to take apart just to check out how they work. I say go for it, but shush, don't let the adults know.

Well, Jeff had an overwhelming need to dismantle stuff; he would take apart anything, much to the shock of people around him, as you will learn in this very interesting chapter about a young experimenter who became a very successful entrepreneur.

Jeff Bezos's Childhood Adventures

Imagine a young boy with dreams as big as the sky, born in a desert city called Albuquerque. This was where Jeff Bezos began his path to greatness, surrounded by landscapes of wide-open spaces and endless possibilities.

Jeff was cared for by his mother and his stepfather, Miguel (Mike) Bezos, who adopted Jeff when he was just four years old, which is why he has his surname.

Jeff's Dad Was an Inspiration

Mike was a mentor and role model to young Jeff, who clearly adored him as he tells the story of how his stepdad came to the US from Cuba at the age of 16 and worked very hard to settle down and pursue a successful career in finance (Tykes, 2022).

His Mom Was an Important Presence in His Life

Jeff Bezos's mom was super important in his life. She always supported his curious nature and let him be adventurous. Whether she was helping him with fun experiments or letting him work on cool projects, her encouragement gave him the freedom to explore. This kind of support helped him ask questions and believe in himself. By allowing him to find solutions to everyday problems, she planted the idea that being creative and solving problems was something he could do—an idea that would later help him with Amazon.

Jeff the Scientist and Explorer

Jeff was not like most children; he enjoyed different experiences and was having a great time turning his backyard into a mini-lab where he did fun experiments and dreamed big.

The beginnings of his great future weren't in fancy offices or schools but in all the cool things he tried out at home. It sounds like so much fun, and I bet he loved playing scientist and trying to create amazing things—maybe even a magic potion that would make him invincible!

Jeff the Surgeon

As a child, Jeff wasn't just playing with toys; he was taking them apart to see how they worked. He was fascinated by gadgets and machines and was often found tinkering in his garage.

He was always asking or thinking, "How does this work?"

Are you like that? Do you ask a lot of questions because you are very curious? If you do, then I think you are on the right track because we learn a lot by asking questions—even if it makes grown-ups groan and roll their eyes, saying you ask a hundred and one questions.

Jeff the Inventor

Jeff didn't learn to love technology from boring classrooms; he was like a superhero of curiosity! Instead of just sitting at a desk, I bet he was busy building robots out of cereal boxes and tinkering

with little gadgets. Imagine a kid who thinks everything can be turned into something cool—like making a robot that can fetch snacks! This playful inventiveness was just the start of Jeff's amazing adventure in creating cool stuff for the whole world.

The Umbrella Solar Cooker

So picture this: Jeff, our super-cool inventor, was super busy tinkering away in his garage lab, kind of like a mad scientist but way more fun! One day, he had a brilliant idea: he decided to turn an umbrella into a solar cooker! Yep, you heard that right—a solar cooker! He thought, "If I cover this umbrella in aluminum foil, I can cook food just by using the sun!"

Now, let's just say that it didn't turn out exactly as he hoped. After cooking some hot dogs—or trying to, at least—he realized that maybe umbrellas weren't the best choice for cooking. But come on, how many kids do you know would even think about turning an umbrella into a cooker? That's pretty wild! It's like saying, "Hey, let's make a pizza using a shoe!" (Spoiler alert: that's probably not a good idea either!)

And that's not all, folks! Jeff was also a genius when it came to protecting his inventing zone—his lab. He created this super sneaky alarm that would sound off whenever his younger siblings tried to sneak into his garage lab. Can you imagine their faces? It was probably like a scene from a comic book! The moment they got close, the alarm went off like a wild siren, and Jeff would be all, "Not on my watch!" Picture him running around, waving his arms, and pretending to be a superhero stopping the evil sibling intruders!

So, Jeff might not have perfected that umbrella cooker, but he sure knew how to have fun and keep his secret lab safe! That's the spirit of a true inventor—always finding a way to turn everyday things into something extraordinary, while having a good laugh along the way!

Jeff the Entrepreneur Kid Organizes a Summer Camp

Jeff's interests didn't stop at technology. Even as a kid, he showed signs of being an entrepreneur—just like Melanie Perkins.

Picture a neighborhood filled with kids during summer. While others played games, Jeff saw an opportunity. He decided to create a summer camp!

He established the camp and came up with fun activities that all the kids in his neighborhood wanted to be a part of, but it wasn't free; the entrepreneur in Jeff showed him how he could make money and offer kids something fun at the same time. So he charged a small fee from everyone who wanted to join his summer camp.

This might look like just some fun kid stuff, but for Jeff, it was like a sneak peek into his future! He was like a mini-boss, organizing games and making everything super fun—proof that he had a knack for business!

Instead of just playing, he was practicing to be a leader while running his little camp. It was like a giant playground with a sprinkle of entrepreneurship! Jeff was testing out his business superpowers and having a blast while doing it!

Smart kid, right? Have you got any ideas like Jeff for summer? Perhaps you too could get together with your friends and organize a summer camp, or maybe some bicycle races, or fun game stalls like the ones they have at fairs.

You could charge a fee from anyone who wanted to join and put that money toward something useful, like your future education, or spend it on helping needy people.

Always Have a Plan—Like Jeff

Guidance is important for young entrepreneurs. If you're thinking about starting your own venture, like a lemonade stand or organizing a fun club with your friends, make sure to consider a few things: start with a plan, be clear on what you want to achieve, and don't be afraid to ask for help when needed. Learn from each experience because every small step is a building block for something greater. When things don't go as planned, reassess the situation and begin again—never surrender!

Jeff's School Life

Jeff's academic years highlight yet another dimension of his extraordinary talents. In school, he excelled, especially in subjects like math and science. Can you see a pattern here, how most tech wizards are good at math and science? What is your strong subject, if you are into tech, then you may be a math whiz even if you don't think so. How about getting serious about your math and science work to show how smart you are?

Jeff the Thinker

Jeff was good at memorizing facts, understanding concepts, and applying them in ways that seemed beyond his years. Jeff would repeatedly memorize concepts and theories, improving his power of memory retention.

Improving memory retention is super important for kids because it helps them learn better and do well in school. When you remember things better, you can understand what you're studying, like math, science, or history, and it makes it easier to finish your homework.

Good memory also helps you remember fun times with friends and family, like birthdays or special events. It can make you better at playing games and sports because you'll remember the rules and strategies. Plus, having a strong memory means you can solve problems more easily and make smart choices.

What Is Understanding Concepts?

Understanding concepts is like solving a fun puzzle! Imagine you have a big box of colorful puzzle pieces. Each piece is a different idea, and when you put them together, they create a picture that makes sense!

Or when you learn something new, like how plants grow, you're taking little pieces of information—like sunlight, water, and soil—and figuring out how they fit together. The more pieces you collect, the clearer the picture becomes.

So, understanding concepts is all about gathering pieces of information, asking questions, and putting them together to create a fun and clear understanding of the world around you!

Here's a fun example for you to understand concepts with the help of AI:

- Step 1: Ask AI to "create a framework for understanding concepts."

- Step 2: Ask AI, "How would this framework work for understanding photosynthesis?"

- Step 3: Using the AI model, apply the framework to understand the concept that interests you.

Check it out and see how simple AI makes tasks.

Jeff the Valedictorian

When Jeff Bezos was in high school, he worked hard and became the valedictorian (Huddleston Jr, 2024), which means he was at the top of his class. The speech Jeff gave as valedictorian was extremely unique and full of dreams. It was even published in the newspaper.

I think you will like what Jeff had to say. The paper article explained his speech by saying that:

Jeff Bezos has a really big dream! He wants to create fun places like space hotels, amusement parks, and even big ships floating in space where millions of people can live. He wanted people to imagine living in a cozy hotel high above the Earth or riding roller coasters floating in space (Huddleston Jr., 2024)! It sounds amazing doesn't it.

The paper also said that Jeff believes that by making these cool places in space, we can help take care of our home, Earth. He thinks that one day, everyone might move to space so that our planet can stay safe and become a giant park for all the plants and animals to enjoy. It's like turning Earth into the biggest playground ever while we have our fun in space (Huddleston Jr., 2024)!

Isn't that just awesome? And what a dream to dream; perhaps one day Jeff Bezos or You may make it happen.

Jeff's Time at University

After high school, he went on to attend Princeton University, one of the world's most prestigious universities. At Princeton, Jeff decided to focus on subjects like electrical engineering and computer science, which are quite technical but also very exciting fields (Dennon, 2021). Especially if you like learning about electrical gadgets and how they work.

Now, you might wonder what electrical engineering and computer science have to do with running a company like Amazon. Well, both subjects teach you how to solve complex problems and think critically, skills that are super important for someone who wants to innovate and create new things. For instance, by learning about computers and how they work, Jeff understood the potential of technology in everyday life. Would you perhaps like to study computer science one day?

The Birth of Amazon

Considering all he had learned from school and his job, Jeff began to dream up a new idea—a platform where people could buy books over the Internet.

He imagined a place where you wouldn't need to leave your home to get your favorite book. After laying down this idea, he pondered over it, realizing it could be much bigger than just books. This idea eventually turned into Amazon, named after the world's largest river, symbolizing the vastness of his vision.

Jeff Made It Big

Jeff Bezos, as of today, is listed among the world's richest people (Srinivasan, 2024)!

Can you imagine that, from tinkering in his garage lab to becoming the world's biggest salesman as Amazon is the world's largest online shop, all Jeff had were big dreams and loads of ambition?

You, too, could dream big and become a huge success like Jeff because dreaming and being determined to achieve his goals are what made Jeff one of the world's greatest entrepreneurs.

Do you have that one cheeky friend who always finds a way to turn simple activities into a great adventure, like the time you guys decided to look for his grandpa's secret stash of sweets perhaps?

Well, our next tech titan liked to think of himself as an unofficial tour guide and was as brave as he could be when chasing his dreams.

Write or draw concepts you would like to explore

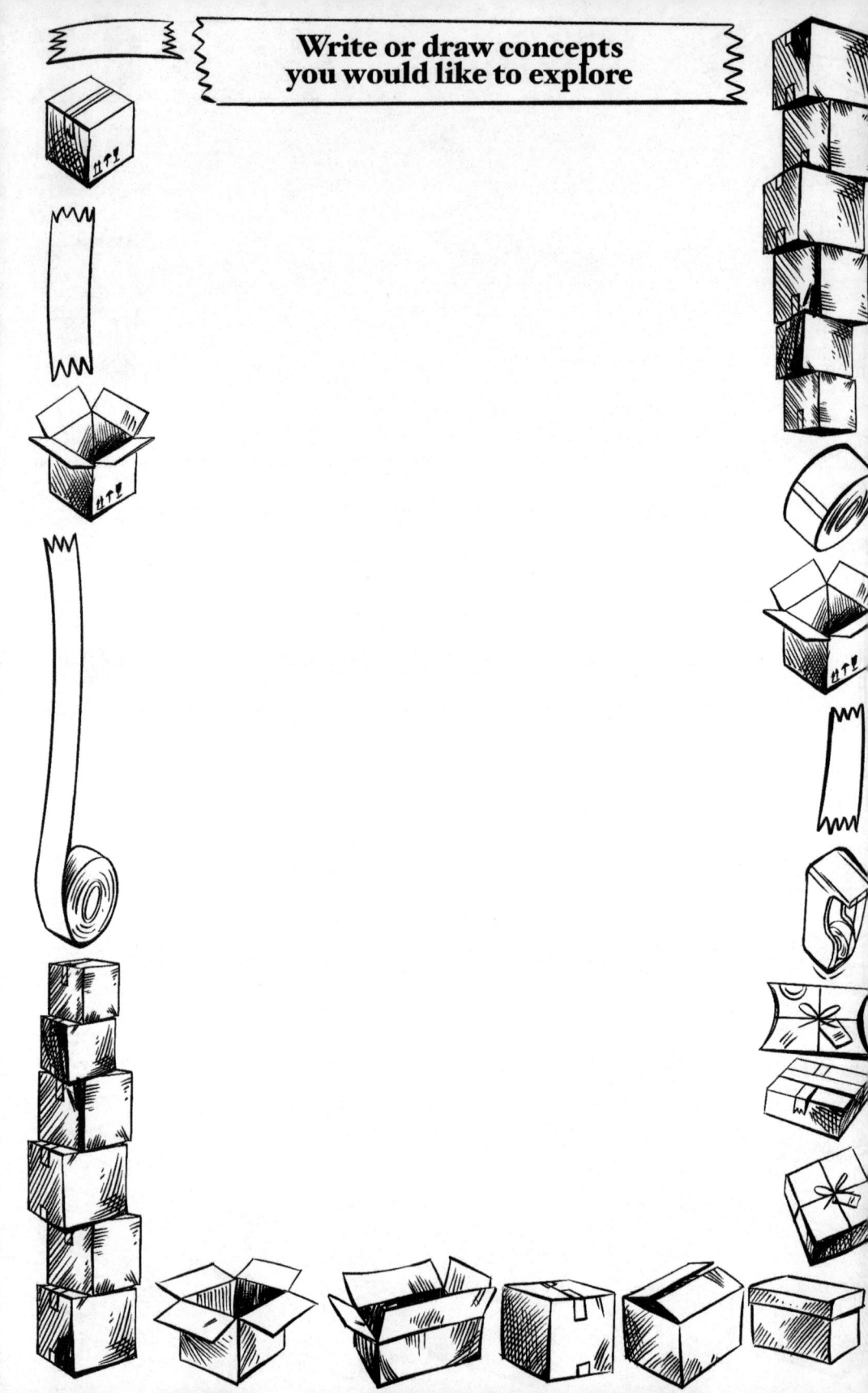

Write or draw concepts you would like to explore

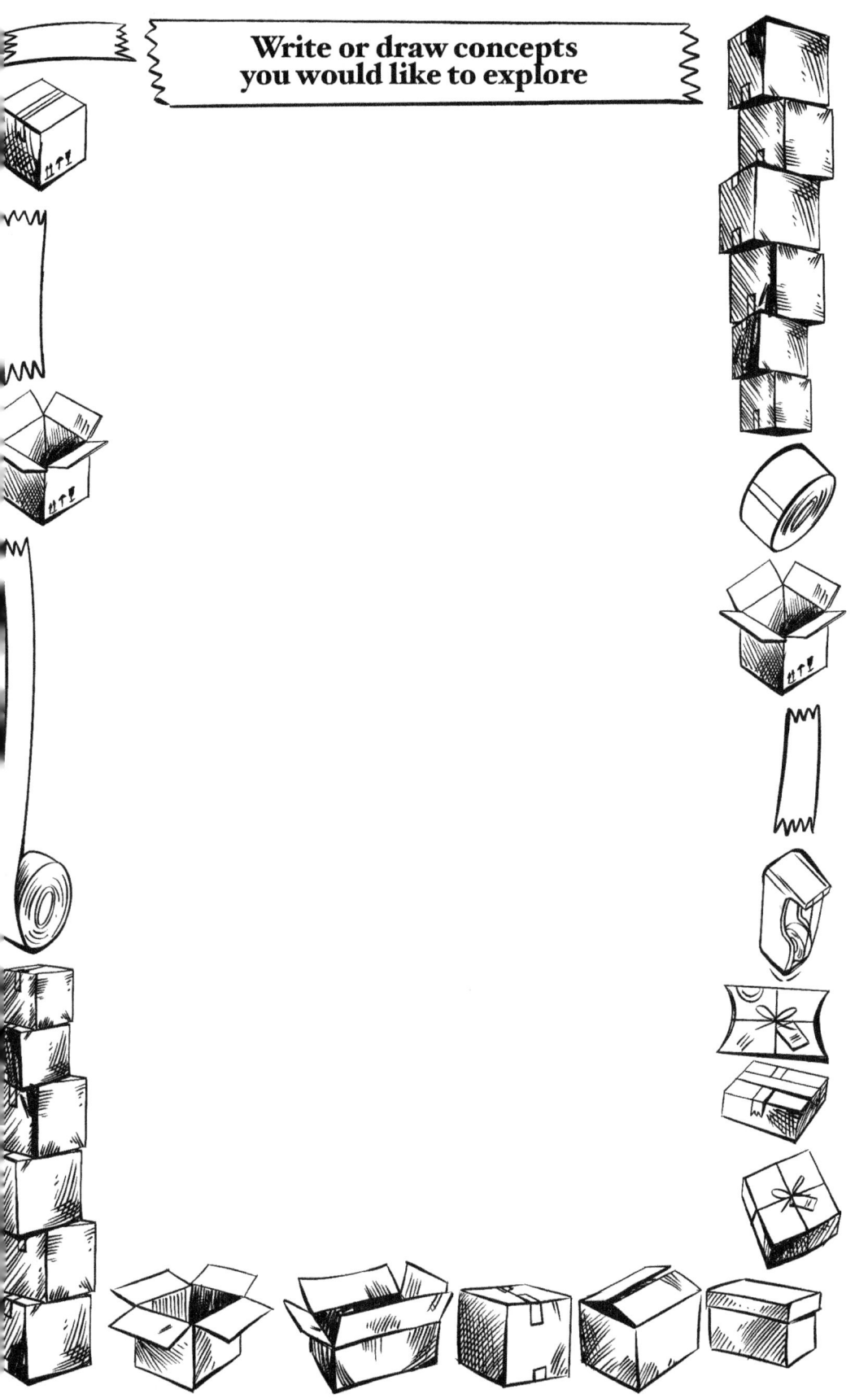

Write or draw concepts
you would like to explore

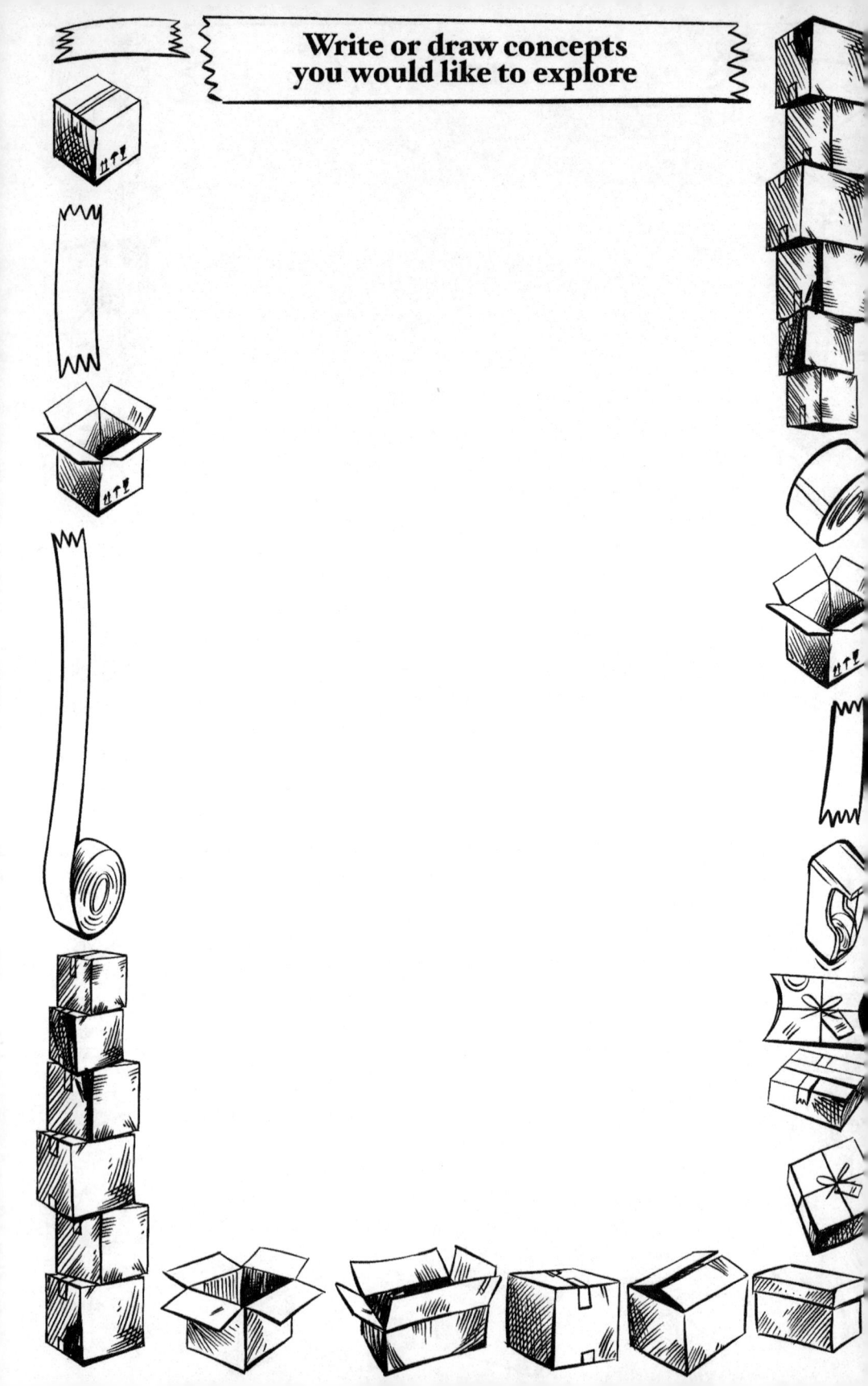

Write or draw concepts you would like to explore

CHAPTER
SIX
JACK MA:
FROM CHALLENGES TO LAUNCHING ALIBABA

Have you heard of Alibaba?

Not Ali Baba and the 40 Thieves, a story about a guy who defeated thieves and found a huge treasure, although it is an interesting story for you to read.

I'm talking about Alibaba, the online store that sells affordable goods to people across the world. Alibaba is a big online marketplace where people can buy and sell lots of different things.

Imagine a huge store that's open all the time and sells everything from toys to clothes to gadgets. People from all over the world can visit this website to find things they need or want, and businesses can also use it to sell their products to customers. It's like having a giant shopping mall right on your computer or tablet! Jack Ma is the tech giant who created Alibaba!

The Story of Ma Yun Aka Jack Ma

Once upon a time in the bustling town of Hangzhou, China, there lived a boy named Ma Yun whose transformation to Jack Ma is like a superhero story, filled with a lot of challenges and a sprinkle of creativity!

As a young boy, Ma Yun faced a lot of bumps in the road, but instead of giving up, he turned those challenges into fuel for his dreams. He had a quirky love for the English language, which made him feel like a mighty explorer ready to connect with the world beyond his hometown, where most people probably did not speak or understand English very well.

Picture Ma Yun as a curious kid in school who didn't always fit in— he was more like a lost sock in a dryer full of pairs! But did that stop him? Nope!

Instead, Ma Yun chose to be clever. He boldly offered free tours to tourists just so he could practice his English-speaking skills. It was this unique approach that became the launchpad for his epic adventures in business.

This chapter isn't just about Ma Yun's transformation into Jack Ma, the entrepreneur; it's a treasure map that shows how even the biggest setbacks can lead to shiny victories. Join Jack, er... Ma Yun, as we follow him through the twisty paths of failure and success, discovering how being tough like your favorite superhero can help you rise again and again!

Jack Ma—The Beginning

Ma Yun was born in Hangzhou, Zhejiang, a city in China. His family was not rich, and he didn't have a lot of fancy things or an easy life growing up. His parents were traditional musicians, who probably did not pay much attention to technology, but like all parents, teachers, and other grown-ups who take care of kids, they encouraged Jack to get an education (Ian, 2024).

Who Are Traditional Chinese Musicians?

Traditional Chinese musicians are artists who play music that originated from China, using special instruments and techniques that have been passed down for many years. They play instruments like the erhu, a type of fiddle, or the pipa, a four-stringed lute. If you are a musician yourself and play the violin or any other, you may want to look up these instruments online to learn more about them.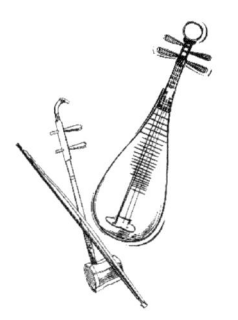

School Life Was Tough

Ma Yun was not the best student in the class and often found some subjects difficult to master. Groan, you may think; I feel for the poor guy!

School wasn't always easy for him, and he struggled particularly with mathematics, a subject vital for many academic pursuits. Ma Yun was not a maths whiz like all the other tech giants we learned about so far—yet he did succeed big time because he focused on his special skill.

Defiance Against Bullies

Jack was smaller in size than others his
age, and because of that, some people were
mean to him and made fun of how he
looked. He was even rejected from simple
jobs at fast food outlets because of how
he looked. But instead of being sad and
giving up, Jack decided to be brave. He
learned how to speak up for himself and
make good deals with others. This special
skill helped him a lot later when he started
his own business!

Giving Up Was Not an Option

Failure did not deter Ma Yun's persistence, meaning he did not give
up. Persistence became his defining trait when he attempted the
college entrance exams twice but failed, and because he did not give
up, he finally succeeded on his third try.

It's a good thing he didn't give up and say, "I suck at college!" He
eventually did get through and managed to get into the Hangzhou
Teacher's Institute, where he majored in his one true love—English
(Ma, 2018). See how focusing on what you love can help you to keep
trying, even if you fail repeatedly.

Jack Ma Embraced English

While at the institute, Ma Yun's interest in the English language took
center stage. He understood that mastering English could be a bridge
to the world beyond China's borders because English is considered a
global language.

English is not spoken in many other countries, and for some people
whose native language is not English, it can be difficult to communicate
when they arrive in countries that speak English as a first language.
However, such factors were not going to stop the future Jack Ma.

By the way, how many languages do you speak?

Perhaps your family originated from a different country, and you
speak English as well as your parents, or grandparent's native

language. If you do, consider yourself special and lucky to have such a varied background.

Ma Yun the Tour Guide

To improve his English skills, Ma Yun came up with a wacky but clever plan! Every morning, he would hop on his bicycle, which was probably more like a superhero's trusty steed, and zoom over to the Hangzhou Hotel. There, he transformed into the town's unofficial tour guide, giving free tours to visiting tourists (Ian, 2024).

Hangzhou where Ma Yun lived, is well known for its natural beauty and is a favorite place for tourists to visit in China, so there were plenty of tourists from all over the world for Ma Yun to show around and chat with.

Picture this: Ma Yun zipping around like a whirlwind, gesturing wildly while trying to show off the coolest sights in town, all while chatting in English, of course! He'd ask tourists questions and happily listen to their stories in exchange for practicing his English. At those moments, he was not a little man that people bullied or rejected; he was an expert guide with interesting stories to tell.

Being a tour guide to people from all over the world opened his eyes to all sorts of cultures and ideas from around the world! So while he was showing off the local sights, Ma Yun was magically turning into a globe-trotting explorer right in his own backyard! Who knew learning could be such an adventure?

These chats were not just about learning a new language. They helped Ma Yun see the world in a bigger way and understand how important it is to talk with people from different places. A nice tourist called him "Jack," and from that day on, everyone around the world knows him as Jack Ma!

Jack Faces More Setbacks

Despite his growing proficiency in English and cultures from across the world, Jack continued to face rejections on his academic path.

His application to Harvard University was turned down 10 times!

Goodness, you may think, but let us also think of how determined Jack would have been to apply 10 times over. Would you do that? Rumor has it he even failed 30 interviews for jobs. Yes, it was a tough life for Jack, but we know he overcame it to become one of the world's richest men (Acharya, 2025).

Jack knew that higher education was key to achieving his dreams and that setbacks were stepping stones in his path forward (Ma, 2018).

After completing his studies, Jack returned to Hangzhou as a teacher in English. His teaching style was both engaging and inspiring, gaining appreciation from his students. I bet he was held in awe by people from his city for turning into this smart fellow who knew a lot about the world.

Founding Alibaba

When Jack Ma started his career, he was an English teacher. Teaching was more than just a job for him; it was the start of an adventure full of surprises! Back then, China wasn't very connected to the rest of the world, but Jack believed that teaching English was about more than just words; it was a way to connect with people and ideas from all around the globe!

During a visit to the US, Jack learned about the Internet or the World Wide Web; it was like magic for him because, in China, the World Wide Web was still not a thing. Returning home, Jack gathered a small group of friends and started Alibaba in his apartment!

At first, it was just a simple website where Chinese small businesses could showcase their products to the world. Unlike traditional stores that charge a lot of money to sell things, Alibaba allows people to sell online without high fees. This made it easier for everyone to join in!

But starting Alibaba wasn't easy! Jack faced many challenges and rejections along the way. Many people didn't believe in his idea and told him it wouldn't work. But instead of giving up, Jack stayed determined. Just like when he was a kid, he believed in his dream and kept pushing forward.

With hard work and a lot of creativity, Alibaba grew and eventually became one of the biggest online marketplaces in the world! Now, people from all over the globe can buy and sell things, all thanks to Jack Ma's vision.

Today, Alibaba has grown and is a platform for buyers and sellers from all over the world to connect, and it has made Jack Ma a very happy, successful, and very rich man.

What do you think?

Being good at math and science isn't the only way to become a successful tech leader.

Although maths and science-whiz kids seem to dominate the world of technology, there are some like Jack whose determination to succeed against all odds, together with a hunger to learn more, does manage to make their dreams come true.

Our next successful tech expert is also a great entrepreneur, who was more into fashion than math and science, let's check her out.

CHAPTER
SEVEN
KATRINA LAKE:
THE STYLISH ENTREPRENEUR

Do you love to dress up in the latest fashion?

Do you dream of perhaps becoming a model or a fashion designer?

If you are interested in fashion and tech at the same time, our next whiz kid is sure to interest you; she is a fashionista with the heart of an entrepreneur.

Just like cheeky young Jack Ma, who appointed himself an unofficial tour guide, our next tech titan is an example that to make it big in the world of technology—having a good sense of fashion and business skills, with plenty of creative ideas—can be a plus point too. Let's learn about a young kid named Katrina Lake.

Katrina Lake's story is a fascinating tale of creativity, determination, innovation, and treating everyone with equality in the ever-evolving world of online retail.

Retail is when stores sell things directly to customers. It's where you go to buy toys, clothes, or snacks. Retailers help people find what they need and make shopping fun!

Katrina had a knack for blending technology with fashion to create something unique and impactful. Her story shows how anyone with a vision and passion can change how we experience everyday things, like shopping for clothes.

Katrina Lake's Entrepreneurial Adventures

Katrina Lake grew up in the vibrant city of San Francisco, California. She came from a very interesting background as her mother spoke only in Japanese and her father in English. Katrina's mother came to the US for studies from Japan, where she met and married her father, a doctor.

Can you imagine having parents who speak to you in different languages? You would be asked to make your bed in two different ways!

Katrina's home became even more interesting when her grandma, too, came to the US from Japan.

I bet there were a lot of stories being told about Japanese traditions while tasty food was being cooked. School lunches were certainly interesting for Katrina and her siblings; some days, it was sandwiches and other days, it was onigiri—yum (Katrina Lake, 2022).

Do you like Japanese food, like sushi?

A lot of people do, and we are lucky that technology has brought the world closer; today, we can experience things like culture and food from different places without having to travel to those countries.

What's your favorite foreign food? Indian, Mexican, American, or Spanish? There are loads to try, isn't it?

Katrina Grew Up as a Mixed-Race Kid

While in San Francisco, Katrina attended a school where most students were Asian, so she didn't feel out of place having parents from different countries.

However, once her family moved to Minnesota, Katrina, who was a teenager then, found she was one of only a few mixed-race kids in school. So she felt out of place and also realized for the first time what it felt like to be a minority.

A minority group is like a small group of superheroes! These are people who might be different from most of the people around them. This difference could be about their skin color, the language they speak, or even their favorite ice cream flavor because who doesn't love a good lobster-flavored ice cream, right? Which, by the way, is a real flavor, check it out!

For example, let's say most kids at school speak English, but there's a group of kids that speak Spanish! They're like the secret agents of language, and they have their own special code!

The important thing to remember is that everyone is unique and special, just like different flavors of ice cream! So, no matter how different someone might be, we should always treat them with kindness and respect. After all, who wouldn't want more friends to share all those delicious ice cream flavors with?

Katrina blended in and made friends; she understood that everyone is important, no matter where they come from or what they look like. And ever since then, has always worked hard to make sure that everyone feels included and welcome. This special way of thinking has played a big part in making Stitch Fix successful!

Do you agree that when we give others space to share their ideas and suggestions, we can make things better? A school project, a play you have to put together, for example, or anything else will always turn out better when we combine different ideas.

The Role Models Who Shaped Katrina's Character

Katrina adored her grandmother, who told her about her great-grandmother and great-grandaunt overcoming many hardships in Japan. They were like superheroes in her life as she listened to amazing stories about how they faced really tough times with a plan and loads of determination.

Surviving World War II, her grandmother had a big dream to live in the United States, so she worked super hard to make that dream come true! After a lot of effort, she was able to send her kids— Katrina's mom and her sister to the US, and eventually, she joined them too! Katrina felt inspired by these incredible women, knowing that if you face challenges with courage and determination, you can achieve anything you set your mind to!

Early Interest in Fashion

Katrina was like a fashion ninja, with a squad of cheerleaders rooting for her, aka her Mom, Dad, and grandma!

As she grew, she discovered her superpower, her fabulous love for fashion! She had a knack for picking out outfits that would make even the dowdiest of her friends look good. Yeah, perhaps she restyled the kid who wore purple pants and a yellow checkered sweater. But Katrina didn't stop at fashion; she also had a passion for technology, like a wizard with cool gadgets.

She loved finding creative ways to mix clothes with the latest tech trends. Imagine her using apps to style her outfits while simultaneously trying to figure out how to make an avatar of a stylish version of herself. She was on a mission to make choosing clothes something special.

This passion for fashion and interest in tech helped her come up with fun ideas for designing special styling experiences with her invention—Stitch Fix!

If you love to experiment with fashion trends by mixing and matching, go ahead and ask your parents or the person taking care of you if you can dress the way you like; who knows, you may start a new fashion trend.

Katrina Enjoyed Various Activities in School

Throughout her childhood and teenage years,

Katrina was actively involved in various activities. She didn't just breeze into school as the best-dressed kid in town.

Katrina was involved in sports and even liked debating, perhaps she was a leader in the debating team and won many arguments because of her strong belief in treating everyone equally.

Her participation in these activities taught her the importance of teamwork and helped her develop a strong sense of discipline, which also helped her on her path toward becoming a great entrepreneur.

A Budding Entrepreneur With an Interest in Business

When Katrina was a kid, she was super curious about how businesses worked. She loved doing fun activities like selling cool things at school; perhaps she sold cookies made from a secret recipe her grandma had. She also got involved in planning school events, showing she had a knack for managing stuff.

Katrina Loved to Read

Katrina Lake was a big fan of reading and loved learning about all sorts of topics, especially business and entrepreneurship. From a young age, she enjoyed exploring books that taught her how to be a good entrepreneur and manage a business.

Reading is an amazing adventure! Books can transport you to magical worlds filled with wizards or dragons, but they also have the power to teach you all about the things you want to understand. For example, you can learn about computers, how they work, and even what a computer virus is and how they're created.

In Katrina's case, the information she found in books helped shape her ideas for starting her own business. She learned about how successful companies operate and what it takes to turn an idea into something real that people can use. Books opened up new horizons for her, helping her think creatively and understand the world of entrepreneurship better.

So, when you open a book, remember that you're not just going on an adventure but also gathering knowledge that could help you in the future! Just like Katrina, you can use what you learn to explore your own interests and maybe even come up with ideas for your future projects or businesses!

Katrina Changes University Degrees

Katrina first attended Standford University, where she started a pre-med course. Yep, Katrina may have wanted to be a doctor like her dad, but along the way, she found business studies kept calling to her, and so after careful thought, she switched and got herself a degree in economics.

She didn't stop there though, Katrina who was super smart, then went to Harvard Business School where she earned a Master's Degree in Business Management, or to be specific she earned a Master of Business Administration (MBA) and also started her very successful online company called Stitch Fix as a student with nothing more than loads of ambition and a target. She didn't have an office, so the company was based at her apartment.

What Is an MBA?

An MBA qualification is like a special badge that grown-ups earn to show they know a lot about running businesses. It helps them learn important skills, like managing people, making money, and solving problems, just like a superhero learns to use their powers!

Here's how someone can get an MBA:

1. First, you must graduate from high school, just like finishing elementary school.

---

2. After high school, attend college and earn a bachelor's degree in a subject you like, kind of like choosing a major to study.

3. Many MBA programs require a test called the GMAT or GRE, which shows how ready you are for business school.

4. Then, apply to different schools that offer MBA programs, telling them why you want to learn about business.

Getting an MBA helps people become really good at their jobs and support their companies in many exciting ways! If you are interested in becoming an entrepreneur like some of the people in this book, don't feel shy about having a plan from your early years.

How Katrina Found Inspiration for Stitch Fix

Katrina got the idea for Stitch Fix when she realized there were a lot of people out there who wanted help with choosing their outfits. She realized that it was a challenge for some people to shop for clothes. So she had an idea to combine technology with personalized styling, leading her to create a platform that delivers specially selected clothing directly to customers' doors. Customers could then select the designs they like and return the rest. It's like having a personal tailor who makes clothes that are prefect for you.

Stich Fix Was a Special Company

Imagine if you and your friends are making a giant pizza together! If everyone brings their favorite toppings, like pepperoni, veggies, and even pineapple, you'll end up with a super yummy pizza that has something for everyone. That's what Katrina did at Stitch Fix!

She made sure to have lots of different people on her team, just like all those fun pizza toppings. When everyone shares their ideas and stories, they can come up with awesome!

Stitch Fix created a friendly place where every person's opinion mattered. It also made the people who worked for Katrina feel important and appreciated; it encouraged them to be creative, which was great for everyone!

Respect Different Opinions—To Learn and Grow

Do you agree it's really important to value everyone's opinion, even if it's different from yours?

Imagine you're playing a team game. Each player has their own ideas about how to win, so when everyone shares their thoughts, you might find some exciting new strategies that you never thought of before!

Listening to different opinions helps us learn new things and see the world in a bigger way. Plus, when we make sure everyone feels heard and appreciated, it makes our friendships and teams stronger. So next time someone has a different idea, remember that it could help you create something really special together! Katrina knew this, and now she is one of the world's richest people and a valued tech giant!

Our next tech titan was responsible for bringing us Netflix! Let's explore his adventure.

Workbook Activity 5: Fashion of the Future

Get ready for an awesome and wildly creative activity that's sure to get your imagination buzzing!

Grab those blank pages at the end of this chapter, and let your artistic flair run free!

Your mission? Design some futuristic fashion trends that you think people will be strutting down the streets 10 to 15 years from now!

Think about wild colors that make your eyes pop, unique patterns that could wow anyone, and super cool, techy accessories.

Could you invent a hat that changes your hair color on command? How about shoes that can adjust their design and height to match your mood—fancy looking for a dance party, flat for a day at the park? We could all own one pair of shoes and be happy!

What do you see in your fashion dreamland? Maybe outfits that change colors based on how you feel, or fabrics so comfy that they keep you cool and fresh all day long, like wearing a cloud made of marshmallows!

Once you've created your fabulous designs, hold onto them like they're treasures! In the future, you can pull them out and see how your predictions stack up against the actual fashion trends—did you hit the nail on the head or go way off into the fashion galaxy? Who knows, maybe one-day, people will recognize your name in the fashion world, just like they do with stars like Katrina Lake!

So, be bold, be imaginative, and let your creativity shine bright like a neon light! Happy designing!

CHAPTER
EIGHT
REED HASTINGS:
A VISION FOR
STREAMING MOVIES

What's your favorite Netflix series?

Do you enjoy spending time on your couch, chilling, and streaming movies with a big bowl of popcorn?

Well, it wasn't always that easy; there was a time when people had to go to movie rental stores and rent the movies they wanted to watch, even having to pay late fees when they were not returned on time.

Thanks to Reed Hastings, today you can stream movies anytime, anywhere. But did you know Reed started out just like you, a kid fighting the ups and downs of school, family life, and other complications that made attaining his dreams a bit harder than usual?

Unraveling the whirlwind journey of Reed Hastings is like diving into a storybook filled with extraordinary adventures and unexpected twists. It's the story of a kid who sold vacuum cleaners door-to-door and volunteered to work in Africa before going off to university!

Reed also loved to take things slow and focus on all aspects of life, such as doing fun things in between working. He was someone who valued education with a humble heart and adventurous spirit.

Are you like that? Do you sometimes dislike planning your days around tight schedules? Rushing from one activity to another, perhaps you have dreams you want to explore and ambitions with studies you want to meet, but you sometimes feel overwhelmed by it all.

Well, by exploring Reed Hastings's story, you may pick up a few tips on how to find a good balance between work and play. After all, he co-founded Netflix, that incredible app that helps us all relax after a long day.

Reed Hastings Childhood Adventures

Reed Hastings was born, in Boston, Massachusetts. He grew up in a middle-class family; his father was a lawyer who encouraged Reed to develop a love for books and explore different genres.

Family life was not always easy for Reed who moved around a lot and had to deal with his parents' divorce. However, the experience taught him to adapt and fit into different situations, which perhaps taught him the value of being flexible and able to adapt to different circumstances. It also made Reed an empathetic person, which helped him become a good leader later in life (Beaver, 2023).

Showing Kindness to Others Makes You Special

Empathy is like wearing someone else's shoes to understand how they feel. If you see a friend who is sad because they lost their favorite toy, empathy means you think about how you would feel in that situation.

When you show empathy, you listen, hug them, or say kind things to help them feel better. It helps us build strong friendships and make the world a nicer place by supporting each other! It also makes you successful in life because being smart at studies and business are not the only keys to success.

Reed Loved to Read

It is believed that as a kid Reed was dyslexic, and while this is a condition associated with a reading difficulty, Reed had an insatiable appetite for reading and would often choose to read books that were way beyond his age! Great books of knowledge and fascinating facts filled his mind with wonder and turned him into a smart young man with a very curious mind.

Do you know kids who are dyslexic?

Dyslexia is like having a special way of thinking and learning. Imagine your brain is like a puzzle, but some of the pieces don't fit together the way they do for others. This can make reading and writing a bit tricky at times.

But here's the cool part: It doesn't mean they aren't smart! Many amazing people with dyslexia have done incredible things! With some extra help, fun tools, and a lot of practice, kids with dyslexia can learn to read and write just like everyone else. Everyone learns in their own way, and that's what makes us all unique and special!

Did you know that Albert Einstein was dyslexic (16 Historic Figures and Celebrities Who Have Dyslexia, 2019)?

From High School to Selling Vacuum Cleaners

Reed attended Buckingham Browne & Nichols School, where he was an average student, not yet a math genius, but Reed was a cool kid, and he decided to take things slow. So, he chose to take a gap year before heading off to college.

Do you know what he did that year? He sold vacuum cleaners.

Hold on now; don't go running off telling your mom you want to take a gap year after high school to become a salesperson. Let's get through middle school first.

Reed was a door-to-door vacuum salesman, but not just any salesman. Imagine a kid knocking on doors and saying, "Hey there! Want a vacuum that can suck up dirt faster than a cheetah on roller skates?"

He must have met all sorts of interesting people along the way. I bet Reed had a blast making new friends and bringing laughter along with his shiny vacuum cleaners!

Read Was a Math Genius in College

Well, after his fun stint as a salesman, Reed excelled in college. He attended Bowdoin College, where he earned a Bachelor's degree in Mathematics. Wow, you may think, but it was his hard work and determination that made it all possible.

Reed Hastings embarked on an exciting school adventure to become a tech superstar! He excelled in College, solving tricky problems like a math wizard.

Reed Attends Standford University

At Stanford, Reed completed his education by studying computer science and artificial intelligence, which is kind of like teaching computers to think! Reed earned a Master's Degree in Computer Science, which is not an easy feat unless you work hard and dream big.

What's a Master's Degree in Computer Science?

A master's degree in computer science at Stanford University is like an advanced class where you learn all about technology and computers. Imagine diving deeper into fun subjects like coding, making computer programs, building apps, understanding data, and even exploring artificial intelligence, which is when computers learn to think and make decisions!

During this program, students work on team projects, solve complex problems, and might even do research, which means searching for new ideas in technology. This helps them become experts in their field.

Once someone finishes this degree, they have many cool career options! They could become software developers who create apps and games, data scientists who analyze information to help businesses grow, or even researchers who work on new technologies. They could also work for big companies like Google or start their own tech businesses! It's a pathway to lots of exciting jobs that shape the future with technology.

Would you like to study computer science one day? It's a good start to a rewarding career in tech.

Reed's Great African Adventure

Remember I told you, Reed Hastings's life was a big adventure because he made sure to broaden his experiences and enjoy different situations.

Well, this is an adventure I'm sure you guys will love to hear about. After college, before attending Stanford University, Reed joined the Marine Corps training program, but before completing that program, he joined the Peace Corps Volunteer program and moved to Africa, where for two years, he taught maths at a village school in Swaziland! How cool is that!

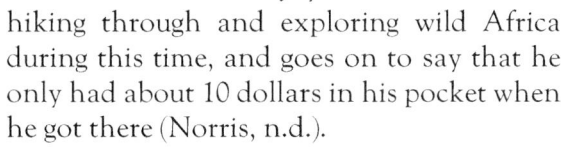

Today, Swaziland is called The Kingdom of Eswatini. There were only 800 students in the school, and I bet a lot of wildlife in the surrounding

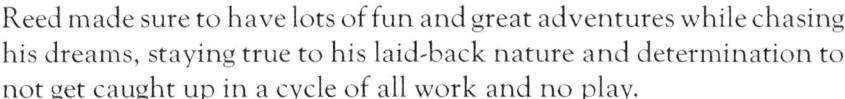

area as well. Reed enjoyed hiking through and exploring wild Africa during this time, and goes on to say that he only had about 10 dollars in his pocket when he got there (Norris, n.d.).

All these exciting adventures, including being a salesman, laid the foundation for Reed to learn about the world and create incredible things, including Netflix!

Reed made sure to have lots of fun and great adventures while chasing his dreams, staying true to his laid-back nature and determination to not get caught up in a cycle of all work and no play.

Do you know what all work and no play means?

"All work and no play" means that if someone spends all their time working and never takes time to have fun, they might become tired or unhappy. It's important to balance responsibilities, like homework or chores, with enjoyable activities, like playing games, going outside, or spending time with friends and family. Just like a car needs fuel to run, sometimes people need fun to feel happy and energized!

Cofounding Netflix

Always an innovator, Reed Hastings founded his first tech company, called Pure Software, after leaving Stanford University. However, it was soon bought over by someone else, and Reed lost ownership—this is something that can sometimes happen in the business world, and it upset Reed a lot.

Then one day, Reed had to pay a $40 fine because he forgot to return a movie he borrowed. That seemed like a lot of money, right? I mean, for just one movie, he could buy a whole snack buffet!

Reed thought about it and had an idea. So he talked to his friend Marc Randolph, and together they created a website called Netflix, but it wasn't the Netflix you know today.

In the beginning, Netflix let people order movies from a list, kind of like ordering pizza. The selected movies were sent by mail on DVD, but it took a few days for them to arrive, which was so slow people might as well have been watching grass grow while waiting for the postman to bring their movie. Imagine waiting for the mail to bring along the next episode of The Loud House, goodness!

At first, Netflix didn't make much money. It was like trying to sell ice cream in winter—hardly anyone wanted it! But Reed and Marc were determined. They came up with a subscription plan, so people had to pay and sign up to rent movies, so they kept coming back for more and found the movie library and recommendation facility offered on the Netflix website very helpful.

Reed didn't stop there; he kept experimenting, looking for ways to make Netflix better. Now, we can stream and watch movies and TV shows anytime on our phones, tablets, or computers! It's like carrying a movie theater in our pockets—just without the popcorn-strewn sticky floors!

Reed Hastings, the Caring Human

There is one more point about Reed Hastings you must know. He values education just as much as he loves his work with Netflix. He believes that school is super important because it can change people's lives for the better. So to make sure underprivileged children had good quality schools to attend, with plenty of modern facilities that offer them equal learning opportunities, Reed started a big fund with $100 million to make schools better all over the United States.

Reed thinks it's important for everyone to get a good education so they can follow their dreams and do amazing things. For him, helping schools isn't just a project—it's something special that he hopes will inspire kids for years to come!

What do you think? Do you believe that Reed Hastings was a truly special person even when he was a kid? He wasn't just really good with technology; he also loved having fun! He understood that both work and play are important. It's like balancing your favorite game with your homework—both can help you grow and enjoy life!

Our next tech titan will teach you that not even getting bullied big time can stop you from becoming a tech whiz!

CHAPTER
NINE
JENSEN HUANG:
REDEFINING THE
FUTURE OF GAMING

Meet Jensen Huang, a tech whiz who admits that as a kid, he never read a single sci-fi book! Eh... you wonder, what would Elon Musk say...

Jensen's story is like a wild adventure! We will explore how he had to grow up super quickly when he arrived in the U.S. without his parents at just nine years old, with only his older brother by his side.

Life in America wasn't easy at first—he faced a lot of bullying, but he learned to be strong and brave. Jensen's journey is all about finding his way and overcoming the challenges that life would throw at him!

Today, we know Jensen Huang as a really smart and creative guy who loves technology and is one of the world's richest people. Jensen is the co-founder of NVIDIA, a cool tech company that makes powerful graphics cards for creating amazing visuals in video games. But they also do a lot more!

Their technology helps with artificial intelligence, data science, and even self-driving cars. Plus, NVIDIA's chips power chatbots like ChatGPT, helping them understand and respond to people. They're all about making computers do amazing things in gaming and tech (NVIDIA, 2019)!

Thanks to Jensen's ideas, we get to enjoy amazing visuals in games and movies that make everything more exciting. So, when you see awesome graphics on your screen, the next time you are playing Minecraft or Shadow of the Tomb Raider, for example, you can think of Jensen and how his curiosity and hard work helped create them!

Jensen, the Kid Who Faced Many Obstacles

Jen-Hsun Huang, aka Jensen Huang, was born in Tainan, Taiwan, to a family that treated education like the coolest adventure ever! Yes, education was very important to his parents, and Jensen learned to study hard from a young age.

His dad was a chemical engineer, like a science wizard, and his mom taught at a grade school, helping curious kids become smart thinkers. They always cheered Jensen on to go after knowledge like it was a treasure, and it really paid off! Jensen's love for learning and hard work helped him become one of the richest tech leaders in the world!

When he was a kid, Jensen loved to play video games; he loved discovering how things worked by taking apart electronics and putting them back together. Even though he had a tough childhood that would make it hard for most people, it's amazing that he grew up to be one of the smartest tech geniuses in the world today!

Jensen's Experiences as an Immigrant

Jensen's family had moved to Thailand, but when the Vietnam War ended, there were problems in the country, as Thailand is close to Vietnam, and Jensen's parents wanted their boys to be safe.

So in 1973, at the age of nine, Jensen and his brother made a big move to the United States alone!

Due to difficulties caused by the Vietnam War, Jensen's parents could not accompany the boys immediately, so they were sent to Tacoma, Washington to live with an uncle.

Imagine jumping into an entirely new world filled with a different language and culture. It was tough because Jensen had to deal with challenges like trying to fit in at school while dodging bullies. But facing these hurdles helped him grow stronger and ready for anything that came his way!

Jensen's Mother the Superstar

Mind you, the brothers could speak and understand English to a certain level when they arrived in the U.S. because their mother, the teacher, had taught them—although she herself did not understand or speak the language, through the use of books, she made them learn 10 general English words every day. Their dedicated Mom made sure her boys were not going to be totally lost in a land that communicated mostly in English.

Jensen's Arrives at a Horrible School

When Jensen and his brother came to the U.S., they met their uncle, but they didn't live with him. He thought he was doing a good thing by sending them to a private boarding school called The Oneida Baptist Institute in Kentucky. But it turned out to be a big mistake because this school wasn't nice at all! It was a reform school for kids who got into trouble, and the kids there weren't treated well.

Since Jensen and his brother were smaller in size and had strong accents, they quickly became targets for bullies. It was a really hard time for them!

Reform schools have teachers and counselors who help kids understand why they might have gotten into trouble and how to change their behavior. However, at the Oneida Baptist Institute, older kids were put in charge of the smaller ones, which did not work well as they bullied and ill-treated the smaller kids.

Jensen Experienced Severe Bullying

Sometimes, it can be hard to understand how tough life can be for other kids, especially when we have safe homes and loving families. But some kids go through really difficult times, just like Jensen and his brother did.

Nine years old, Jensen had to share his boarding schoolroom with a 17-year-old boy who showed him some scars on his chest and warned him about knife fights at the boarding school. That must have made Jensen feel really scared! But he was a clever kid. He offered to help teach his older roommate to read if, in return, the roommate could teach him how to do bench presses (Witt, 2023).

Jensen later talked about how most kids at the school carried little knives and smoked cigarettes, but he and his brother had to remain silent since their parents were not there for them to ask for help; instead, they chose to stay away from trouble as much as possible. It shows that even in hard situations, it's important to make good choices and help each other out, although remaining quiet about getting bullied is not a good idea because seeking help from someone you trust when you have the option, can make a bad situation better.

Jensen Meets Ben Bays and Encounters More Bullying

Although, Jensen was boarded at the Oneida Baptist Institute, he was too young to attend classes there, so he ended up going to a public school filled with kids who didn't have much. There he met a boy named Ben Bays, who became his friend. Ben's family was struggling so much that their house didn't even have running water!

But even public school wasn't easy for Jensen. He was often bullied there, too, because he looked different, and the other kids called him rude names. Instead of letting it get him down, Jensen decided to be brave. He remembered crossing a shaky old footbridge with missing wooden planks on his way to school. The older boys would wait for  him to get halfway across and then rock the bridge, trying to scare him and make him fall into the river!

But Jensen, like a true hero, didn't let their tricks get to him. He focused and expertly made it across that crazy bridge without a scratch. Over time, the older boys began to respect Jensen for his bravery, and they eventually became friends. Soon enough, Jensen was leading them on exciting adventures playing in the nearby woods, proving that sometimes courage and friendship can grow in the most unexpected places! Don't you think Jensen was a very brave boy to survive all that?

Jensen Does Amazing Things

Jensen's school years were like a wild adventure! First, his parents finally made it to the U.S., and when they saw how their boys were living, they quickly moved them to a cozy family home in Oregon. This new place was way safer, and it helped Jensen settle down and discover his amazing genius! It was the perfect chance for him to dive into learning and become the smart tech whiz he is today!

Jensen, the Star Athlete

In high school, he was not just a bookworm; he was also a table tennis champ! Jensen considered it important to balance his studies and sports like a real professional and even became nationally ranked in ping pong, which is another rather funny name for table tennis. Aren't you glad Jensen didn't allow his rough start in the U.S. to spoil him, he could have ended up on a bad path, but instead he stuck to his goals, and decided to fight for what he believed was right

Jensen Excelled in High School

Guess what? This amazing kid wasn't just a super athlete; he was a whiz at academics too! Jensen didn't just play sports—he jumped right into science, math, and computer clubs at school! He worked so hard in school that he actually jumped ahead two whole grades—how cool is that?

By the time he was just 16 years old, Jensen graduated from high school! Talk about zooming along the fast track to success! Jensen was not just a star athlete, he was a total Rockstar in the classroom too! Would you like to skip to jump a grade or two? Won't that be amazing?

Jensen in University

After graduation, Jensen headed to Oregon State University to study electrical engineering. There he came across a rather nerdy-looking girl with curly hair, no he did not make fun of her, he liked her very much, and today that girl, Lori Mills is his

wife. Aw, I bet you are blushing now, but don't you think this kid deserved the best after all he went through?

What Is Electrical Engineering?

Studying electrical engineering in university means learning how to understand and create things that use electricity! You'll figure out how gadgets like smartphones and robots work, design circuits (which are like roads for electricity), and solve problems with power and electronics. It's like being a superhero for technology, helping to make our devices work better and invent new cool things! If you love science, math, and gadgets, it could be a really fun adventure!

Jensen's Path to Success

With a great education, Jensen jumped right into Silicon Valley, where he started designing microchips. He also got married to Lori and went to night school at Stanford to earn his Master's Degree in Electrical Engineering. It was an exciting time in his life!

Ready to make a difference in tech! He kicked off his career at Advanced Micro Devices (AMD), and that's when he had a major lightbulb moment about computers creating amazing graphics. Teaming up with other innovative minds, he co-founded NVIDIA and became its Chief Executive Officer or CEO at just 30 years of age.

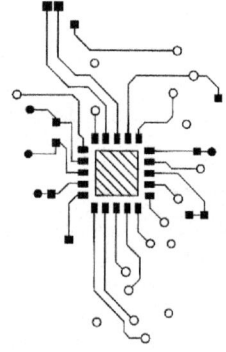

NVIDIA is a company that reshaped how we see computer graphics today and is tipped to be one of the coolest places to work, thanks to its amazing co-founder Jensen Huang. At first, the company focused on graphics technology. Their goal was to make powerful graphics processing units (GPUs) that could handle the needs of video games and high-quality graphics.

NVIDIA hit a big milestone when they launched the RIVA series of graphics cards. As more and more people got into gaming and cool computer graphics, NVIDIA's products became super important for gamers and game makers. Over the years, the company kept coming up with new ideas and improving its technology, making it a leader in gaming, artificial intelligence, and data science.

What Is Silicon Valley?

Silicon Valley is a special place in California known for technology and innovation! It's home to many amazing companies that create cool things like smartphones and video games. Picture it as a giant playground for inventors, engineers, and entrepreneurs where smart people work together to turn their ideas into reality and start companies. If you dream of being a programmer or an inventor, Silicon Valley is where a lot of that magic happens, making it an exciting spot for anyone who loves technology, as it is home to tech companies like Apple, Facebook, NVIDIA, Netflix, Tesla Engineering and other top businesses.

Did You Like the Story of Jensen Huang?

Jensen believed that computers could be used for more than just tasks—they could create amazing visuals and change how we interact with technology. This idea led him to co-found NVIDIA, teaching us that staying curious and open-minded can lead to great things, and by learning and adapting, anyone can achieve their dreams.

Even though he had a tough life as a kid, it did not stop him from achieving great things. Do you think you could be that brave and determined?

Let's move on to our next tech giant, a great entrepreneur who brought us Dell computers! Yes, you guessed right.

Fun Activity 5: "Silicon Valley Here I Come"

Step 1: Imagine you are going to Silicon Valley; make a list of four or more ideas you want to develop there.

Here are some cool ideas for you to get started:

Gaming App: Create a fun mobile game that combines learning with play, like a trivia game that teaches math or science.

Robot Helper: Design a robot that helps with chores or homework. It could have fun features like voice commands or learning games.

Eco-Friendly Invention: Develop a gadget that helps save energy or reduces waste, like a smart recycling bin that sorts waste automatically.

Virtual Reality Learning: Create a virtual reality experience that teaches kids about history, science, or art, making learning feel like an adventure.

Interactive Storytelling App: Build an app that lets kids create and share their own stories, complete with choices that change the ending.

Smart Homework Assistant: Invent an app that helps kids organize their homework, set reminders, and find study resources in a fun way.

Step 2: Use AI to find out the skills you must develop to develop these inventions and take them to Silicon Valley.

Here's an example of a search term you can use on an AI chatbot:

"What skills will a 12-year-old need to develop to invent a smart homework assistant app?"

Use blank pages after this chapter to write down your ideas and skills that you want to develop.

Happy inventing!

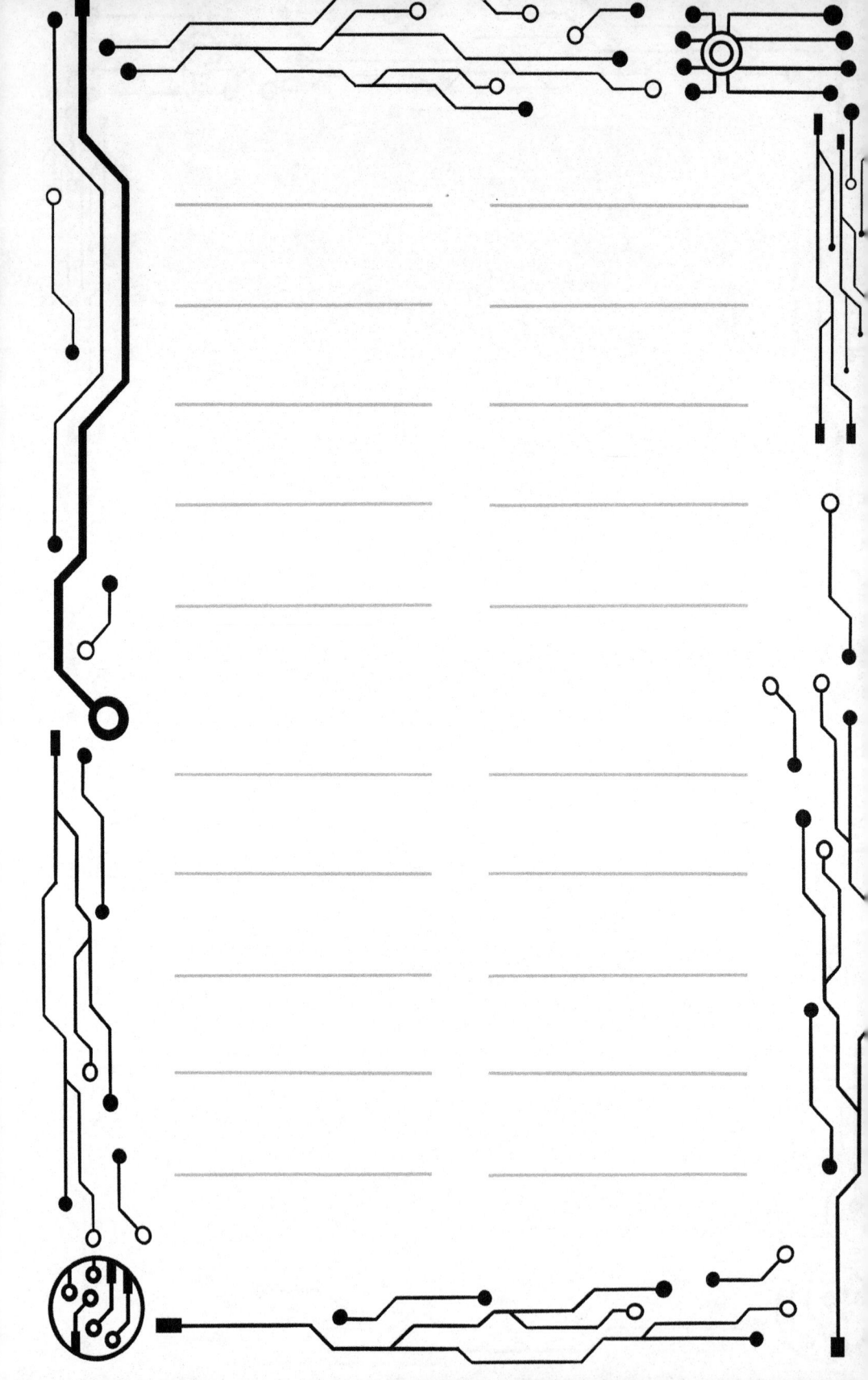

CHAPTER TEN

MICHAEL DELL:
TURNING CURIOSITY INTO A COMPANY

Do you own a laptop? Or a desktop computer? Perhaps you borrow your parents' computer to complete your homework and other projects.

Or maybe you have an older brother who owns a cool and very powerful Dell G Series gaming laptop, complete with a NVIDIA® GeForce RTX™ graphics cards! Which you aren't even allowed to touch!

Our next tech titan, Michael Dell, is the man behind Dell Technologies, a company that creates laptops and other high-tech gadgets to help people and businesses stay connected, work better, and play games using computers and storage systems.

Turning curiosity into a company is the fascinating journey of Michael Dell. A reserved boy from a young age, Michael exhibited an inquisitive nature that led him to dismantle household electronics to understand their inner workings. He always asked questions and found ways to make gadgets better. Michael was interested in technology from a young age, and he even took apart his computer just to see how it worked!

He also had a special ability to come up with great money-making ideas, which is what we call being an entrepreneur. When he was younger, he tried different activities, like selling newspapers and trading stamps with his friends. Michael loved to create and come up with new ways to make things happen, and that passion helped him grow into the successful businessman he is today!

Michael Dell's Childhood

Michael Saul Dell was born in Houston, Texas. His father was an orthodontist and encouraged his son to follow medicine; his mother was a stockbroker, and perhaps that's where he got his business skills.

An orthodontist is a special type of dentist who focuses on fixing teeth and jaws to help people have straighter smiles.

However, Michael, a shy kid, showed an early interest in technology and entrepreneurship. As a child, he began dismantling household electronics to see how they worked. This curiosity was more than simple play; it was an early sign of his interest in innovation, which would later define his career path. By taking apart radios and other devices, Michael Dell learned about their mechanics, laying the groundwork for his technical prowess.

Michael Dell, the Budding Entrepreneur

When Michael was just 12 years old, he became interested in business when he started a new venture—trading stamps. His stash included collectible stamps, which are stamps valued for their artistic of historic value and postage stamps, which are stamps that have been on an envelope that was mailed and therefore have a post office seal on them. Collecting stamps was a popular hobby back then, and lots of kids collected different types of stamps.

He mainly focused on stamps that had value to collectors, which often included stamps with rare or unique designs. It might sound small, but for the 12-year-old boy, it was a big deal. He learned how much different stamps were worth and how to buy and sell them. He was so passionate about growing his stamp collection that he got a part-time job as a dishwasher at a local restaurant to earn money to buy more stamps.

This helped him understand how business deals work. Trading stamps taught him a bunch of important skills, like how to keep track of costs and make money. It also made him think about money and how to use it wisely. These early experiences helped him become really smart about business, getting him ready for bigger things in the future!

What do you collect? Stamps or Pokémon cards?

Perhaps not stamps, it's no longer a popular hobby, mainly because we rarely use regular postal services. But stamp collecting for some kids who still do is very rewarding, especially when you get to trade them with other collectors. You can ask your grandparents or any other older adult you know about stamp trading back in the day to understand the hobby better.

A Curious Boy Builds His First Computer

Here's a cool fact: When Michael Dell was just 15 years old, he got an Apple Computer and had a brilliant idea! Instead of just using it, he took it apart to see how it worked, and then he put it back together. I guess it worked fine, too, after that. Now, don't you go taking apart your Dad's expensive Apple computer, or is it a Dell laptop?

This awesome experiment taught Michael a lot about computers. So, later, when he was in university, he started fixing and selling broken computers, showing off his tech skills and entrepreneurial spirit. Talk about a tech whiz with a passion for business!

Michael Buys His First Car

As a teenager, Michael's amazing talent for business really started to shine.

When he was just 16 and in high school, Michael found work selling subscriptions for the Houston Post newspaper. To build a good base, he came up with a clever plan to focus on newly married couples and new homeowners, who probably hadn't ordered their subscriptions yet. Smart right? This smart idea helped him find a brand-new group of customers, and his sales took off!

It's reported he made $18,000 in one year (Stone, 2014b)! Over $60,000 worth of money today—wow! With the money he made, Michael very happily bought his first car. He felt proud that he set goals and made them happen by working hard.

This early experience taught him important lessons about marketing and connecting with customers. He realized that to make people happy, you need to understand what they want, just like putting together a cool puzzle where every piece has to fit just right! This skill would become super important for his future business adventures!

The Deli Job

In high school, apart from selling newspapers, Michael Dell took on a part-time job at a local deli, and let me tell you, this wasn't just about making sandwiches! He learned a ton about customer service by talking to people every day. Imagine trying to remember everyone's favorite sandwich order—it's like being a superhero with a super memory!

Michael noticed that when the deli gave customers extra attention and made them happy, they kept coming back for more sandwiches. This taught him that businesses grow by really listening to what customers want—like maybe a sandwich with extra pickles!

Working at the deli also helped Michael learn important skills like talking to people, showing kindness, and being patient, especially when someone couldn't decide between turkey or ham. These valuable lessons stayed with him and shaped his future, helping him build Dell Technologies with a big focus on what customers need and want. Who knew making sandwiches could lead to such a tech empire?

Michael's University Experience

Have you sometimes done things to make someone happy, even though it was not something you really wanted to do—like making your bed and tidying up your room; you may not like it, but it sure would make your Mom happy, so you do it anyway, right?

Well, Michael did something like that when he joined the University of Houston, Texas as a pre-med student of biology. Okay, by now, we all know this kid is really only interested in computers and business. But just like his father wanted him to, he gave medicine a shot.

Guess what, ever the entrepreneur, Michael did not waste his time in Uni—while studying medicine, he kept a side hustle going by upgrading and selling computers from his dorm room. He was so successful that in his first year, he made $80,000 from those computer sales (Academy of Achievement, 2023).

After just his freshman year at the University of Houston, Texas, Michael Dell realized that sitting in classes learning about biology wasn't quite as exciting as building computers. Imagine trying to pay attention to a long lecture while dreaming about the cool computers you could make instead!

And so, Michael never returned to university after his freshman year, go figure! He ended up dropping out after his first year without completing his major in Biology; he had bigger dreams than becoming a doctor.

Founding Dell Technologies

Back then, computers were still new and exciting, and Michael had an idea. He realized that no one was selling computers directly to customers—talk about a missed opportunity!

So, instead of following the usual way and going through stores, he took a leap of faith and used $1,000 from his savings (his secret stash for video games, maybe?) to start building and selling computers to his college buddies, which laid the foundation for Dell Technologies to be born.

But Michael wasn't just about making awesome machines; he also wanted to treat his customers like rock stars, giving them great support and prices that wouldn't break the bank. Before long, his little gig grew, and he started getting orders from people outside of school. He got so busy that he decided to drop out of university and go all in on his computer business—imagine telling your teachers you're off to be a billionaire instead!

After dropping out of university, Michael formed PCs Limited and, together with a few buddies, started selling computers directly to customers. Sales were very good, so Michael then founded the Dell Computer Corporation in 1984, and guess what? In its first year, Dell Computer Corporation raked in a whopping $6 million (Tucker, 2023)! Can you believe it?

Time flew, so did sales at Dell and by 2001, Dell Corporation became the biggest PC maker in the world, beating then-leader, Compaq

(Dell Technologies, 2023)! It's like going from selling cookies on the playground to running the coolest cookie factory ever! What a ride!

Hey, kids, what do you think about Michael Dell's awesome story? He was a shy kid who loved playing with computers and thinking of smart business ideas. Even though he wanted to make his parents happy, he followed his dreams and became a billionaire and a creator in the world of personal computers.

Do you sometimes wish you could easily find stuff—clothes, books, that missing sock? Our next tech titan was a whiz at creating computer programs that help put information in order. Let me introduce you to the inventor of the Oracle.

CHAPTER
ELEVEN
LARRY ELLISON:
RESILIENCE IN ORACLE'S
JOURNEY

Meet Larry Ellison, a super cool tech wizard who helped create Oracle, a company that makes amazing software!

Imagine you have a giant toy box filled with all your favorite toys, but it's a total mess, and sometimes, finding that special toy can feel impossible, right?

Well, Larry's company makes computer tools that help businesses organize their information called data because sometimes managing a load of data can also become messy for companies—like your toy box or room. Like a magical toy organizer that finds what you need in a snap, the Oracle Database Management System, which Larry Ellison helped create, makes finding information for businesses superfast (Beaver, 2023b)!

What Is Company Data?

Company data is like a treasure chest filled with important information that helps businesses understand how they're doing so they can make smart decisions.

Imagine a toy store that keeps track of everything it sells. Each time someone buys something, that information goes into a big notebook aka database, like what toys are most popular, how many customers visited the store, and even how much money they made.

This data can be numbers, such as how many products were sold, or facts, like what customers said they liked or didn't like about a particular toy. By looking closely at the data, the store can figure out things like which toys have the most demand to stock up on more, which promotions work best, and how to serve their customers better depending on reviews and how well the store did in terms of sales. So, company data, which is sorted into different sections, is super important because it helps businesses understand their success, find out what people want, and make plans for the future!

Larry's adventure began when computers were just becoming popular, which is really exciting! But here's something amazing: He was dyslexic, which means he had a tough time with reading and writing in school, and it did not stop him from becoming one of the biggest tech innovators of all time.

Even with challenges, he didn't give up, and his story shows that you can overcome obstacles and achieve great things, no matter what. So, get ready to dive into Larry's inspiring story and discover how his passion for technology, resilience, and fierce need for independence changed the world!

Larry Ellison's Early Life and Challenges

Born in New York City, Larry was given up for adoption by his mother, who was only 19 years old and a single parent. He was adopted when he was just nine months old by his mother's aunt and uncle, Louis and Lillian Ellison.

Larry did not know he was adopted at first; he found out when he was around 12, but although he knew who his biological mother was, he never met his biological father.

These realizations made him a sort of rebel and also fiercely independent and self-reliant—which means he relied mostly on himself. Although Larry reacted badly to his adoption and may have encountered feelings of abandonment, being adopted for most kids is a good thing; it can help kids find loving families who can take care of them better.

At first, Larry Ellison's family did not have much money to spend on anything other than the basics, and he faced some tough challenges that taught him the importance of being strong and determined to make his way in the world. Instead of letting challenges hold him back, Larry used the difficulties as a stepping stone to becoming more focused and ambitious about what he wanted to do.

Larry Didn't Get On With His Dad

Larry's relationship with his adoptive parents was strained, it is believed that his father would often make him feel inadequate, fuelling his rebellious streak, which often led to arguments with his father.

Larry's relationship with his mother was different, she was a strength to him and would constantly encourage him to believe in himself. It may have been this relationship that kept Larry focused on his goals instead of giving up. These are probably reasons why, from an early age, he understood that to succeed, he had to face challenges directly and turn tough times into chances for growth.

Larry Was Diagnosed With Dyslexia

A significant challenge that shaped Larry's educational path was his diagnosis of dyslexia. The learning disorder made traditional schooling difficult for him, as his mind processed information differently from other students. He often found it hard to keep up with the school curriculum, which frequently made him feel frustrated and left out.

However, Larry, a tough cookie, did not give up; he embraced unconventional learning approaches. For example, he found that he learned better by doing things his way and getting involved in experiences instead of just memorizing lessons.

One important aspect of Larry's childhood was discovering a talent for self-learning, especially about tech-related stuff, as a way to cope with his dyslexia. Instead of relying solely on traditional teaching methods, he took charge of his education, exploring topics that interested him.

This approach allowed him to learn at his own pace and delve deeper into subjects that caught his attention. This, in turn, helped him realize that he had a deeper talent for technology and even taught himself computer programming, which set him on the right track toward becoming an innovator in the world of tech.

Larry found it hard to learn in regular school, showing that everyone learns differently. Sometimes, struggling in school can make kids feel like they can't do great things. But Larry's story shows that these struggles can make you stronger and more determined to succeed. It's important to understand that everyone has their own way of learning, and what helps one person might not help another. Trying different ways to learn can help you reach your dreams and achieve amazing things.

Larry's Talent for Tech Shines Through

Larry Ellison's transition to becoming a tech giant is rooted in his early curiosity about technology. Although he dealt with dyslexia, he understood tech from an early age and was fascinated by how things worked. He spent countless hours tinkering with gadgets, taking them apart, and putting them back together—as most of our tech titans did! This inquisitiveness laid the groundwork for his later ventures in technology, as it helped him develop a strong understanding of computer systems and problem-solving skills.

Mentors Played an Important Role in Shaping Larry

While traditional schooling posed difficulties, mentors in the form of dedicated teachers and his adoptive mother provided invaluable support to Larry, often tailoring their approaches to suit his learning needs. These mentors didn't just teach him academic subjects; they encouraged him to think critically and creatively, allowing him to thrive and embrace his differences.

Mentors can offer guidance and support even during the hardest challenges you face. They can inspire and challenge you to not give up, leading to personal growth and new opportunities.

Larry Drops Out of University

A self-taught tech whizz, Larry never graduated; he did attend university, though—twice. The first time he joined the University of Illinois in Urbana Champaign. However, he dropped out after just two years when his adoptive mother passed away.

Larry later joined the University of Chicago but soon quit and moved to California, where he worked as a computer programmer for several different companies. It was during his time working for various tech companies, where he even went on to become vice president of one, that Larry met the other co-founders of Oracle. Together they saw a need for streamlined data sorting, and so Larry, along with his friends Bob Miner and Ed Oates, created a tool for businesses to sort out their data that would be faster and better than what was available at the time.

They came up with the idea of a database, which would be a super-smart filing cabinet for information, and founded the Oracle. Oracle's database software became very popular, and over the years, Larry Ellison worked hard to make Oracle a big success. It wasn't all smooth sailing; there were good times and bad, but Larry, who had made it through several challenges like a tough young man, was never going to give up.

He was known to be a strong leader who would push everyone to be their best, and now Oracle is one of the largest technology companies in the world—recognized as revolutionizing data sorting software!

Larry Ellison's story is like a superhero origin tale, showing how even the roughest beginnings can lead to something awesome if you stick to your dreams and eat your veggies—just kidding, but you get the idea! Instead of letting dyslexia trip him up, Larry decided to become a computer whiz all on his own. He tackled family challenges like a boss and figured out how he learned best. His childhood adventures are packed with lessons on bouncing back, being independent, and putting on your tough pants when life gets wobbly.

Today, that kid who once had a hard time reading, dealt with a messy family situation, faced letdowns, and felt like the odd one out is now one of the richest and coolest tech geniuses around!

So, what do you think? Isn't it amazing how it's not about what happens to you, but how you roll with the punches that counts? Remember, every superhero has to face their challenges—just make sure to have a good snack along the way!

Our next tech titan is also a Larry! Go ahead and Google him!

CHAPTER
TWELVE
LARRY PAGE:
A SEARCH FOR KNOWLEDGE
THAT CREATED GOOGLE

What do you know about Google? Other than searching for your favorite cartoons, game series, or your favorite celebrity?

Well, in a nutshell, Google is like a giant, magical library that's always open and ready to help you find answers to just about anything!

Maybe your Google account is controlled by your parents because Google offers parents the option to do so—recognizing that there is some information that young minds are not ready to process. So you will have access only to what's important and fun for you.

The information you can access on Google is loads of fun. Imagine it like a super-smart friend who knows the secrets of the universe but also has a collection of funny cat videos you enjoy watching.

Google can help if you want to know how to make a cool volcano for a science project or tell you what the fastest animal in the world is; you just type your question into Google, and voilà! It's like having a magical genie that pulls out all the answers without any smoke or mirrors—just a lot of links and pictures!

But hold on, it does even more than just search!

Need directions to the nearest ice cream shop? Google's got you covered. Want to know if you should wear a raincoat or a swimsuit tomorrow? Google can tell you! Plus, it can help you send emails, play games, and find out interesting facts about your favorite superheroes. So, think of Google as your super-smart  buddy who's also superfast—just don't ask it to help you with your math homework unless you want the answer to be even more confusing!

 Larry Page's search for knowledge and his love of collecting information were key ingredients in the creation of Google. Yes, he is one of the guys responsible for this amazing online library of endless information.

Imagine being a kid with an unending curiosity and a big collection of gadgets to explore—that was Larry Page, always tinkering and learning. From dissecting household electronics to diving into books about science and technology, Larry's childhood was like a treasure hunt for knowledge.

This chapter takes you through his early life, revealing how his surroundings helped shape a brilliant mind that would later co-found one of the world's most famous companies. Oh, and last I heard, it's one of the coolest places to work—just Google it and see.

Larry's Fascinating Childhood

Born in East Lansing, Michigan, Larry dived into a super cool world filled with brains and tech magic! His family was like a legendary team of smartypants, and it was clear they were supporting him for greatness in the tech universe.

Larry's Family Were Super Smart Heroes

Larry's childhood was like a sneak peek into a science fiction adventure. His dad, Carl Page, was a computer science professor at Michigan State University, which was a big thing since back then, computers were just starting to become popular, and only a few special people were computer whizzes.

So, while other kids were talking about cartoons, Larry was having dinner conversations about the coolest tech breakthroughs with his parents because, guess what? His mom, Gloria Page, was also a programming whiz! With both parents in the tech game, Larry's home was like an epic training ground that set him up to become a superstar in computer science! (Ramanathan, 2024).

Larry, the Young Tech Genius

From a young age, Larry was like a curious little squirrel on a mission, always eager to learn and explore! While other kids were busy playing with action figures and dolls, Larry had a different idea of fun—he thought gadgets were way cooler! To him, computers were like magical toys that made his imagination go wild.

His brother, the self-proclaimed "King of Dismantling," taught him the fine art of taking apart everything around the house. Want to know what happens when you open up the toaster? Larry did! With a screwdriver in hand, he discovered all the mysterious bits and pieces inside, which made him feel like a superhero tinkering in his lab. These hilarious adventures not only satisfied his creative cravings but also turned him into a tech wizard who couldn't wait to invent the next big thing!

The influence of having access to computers when Larry was a kid was a rare treat. At that time, which was around the late 1970s and early 1980s, computers were not found everywhere as they are today. However, thanks to his father's passion for the subject and willingness to invest in new technology, Larry was able to play around with a computer at home from around age six. This was at a time when only a few of his friends had even heard of computers He was probably the only child in his elementary school turning in word-processed homework assignments, which he did with the help of his brother— so you see the entire family were tech geniuses who greatly supported Larry on his path to greatness.

Larry Enjoyed Reading

Does your family love to read? Perhaps your mom or dad has a collection of books from their favorite author, your older sibling has a fascinating series of books on sci-fi, or maybe there's a library close by to your home or school that you like to visit. Well, Larry's home environment nurtured his spirit of inquiry and creativity as there was plenty to read about science, tech, and other fascinating subjects. The Pages' home was filled with books and magazines like Popular Science, sparking further curiosity in young Larry, who spent hours lost in those books.

The books and magazines provided him with endless material to fuel his imagination, helping him realize that inventing things through the computer wasn't just fun but also something that could lead to significant breakthroughs. With this knowledge, he understood the importance of creating and also bringing inventions to life in practical ways that could benefit others, and by age 12, Larry already knew he wanted to start his own company someday (American Academy of Achievement, 2022).

Larry the Musician

Larry wasn't just lost in the world of tech; he enjoyed music and studied music composition, saying music had a huge influence on his tech inventions. Just like Steve Jobs, who enjoyed calligraphy, Larry found music made him a better tech whiz.

During summer break, his parents sent him to music camp. He attended the Interlochen Center for the Arts for two summers, where he learned to play the saxophone and flute.

Larry says that learning about music taught him patience when it came to designing his computer programs, it also made him realize that time was super important because music is based on precise timing—kind of like the drummer who has to deliver the beats and hit the clash in a flash at exactly the right moment. You know the guy in the band who sits quietly at his drums but suddenly goes crazy and delivers a series of beats and clashes at one precise moment. Just like that quick reaction based on timing, Larry believes that his music training helped him create Google as a superfast search engine.

Larry's folks didn't just talk the talk; they walked the walk! They showed Larry that using your smarts to make the world a better place is a superpower in itself. They encouraged him to explore all his talents so he could combine them and gain a more comprehensive understanding of what he needed to do.

Watching their dedication inspired Larry to dive headfirst into his passions, like a superhero leaping into action! And guess what? With dedication and a sprinkle of fun, he zoomed all the way to remarkable achievements in the tech industry!

So, if you ever feel like your dreams are out of reach, remember Larry's story! With a little inventiveness, a dash of humor, and a whole lot of passion, you can achieve anything you set your mind to! Now, go out and don't feel discouraged to embrace the amazing inventor you were meant to be!

High School and University

Larry graduated high school and entered the University of Michigan, where he graduated with honors, earning a Bachelor of Science in

Computer Engineering. During his time at Michigan University, Larry came through as a genius inventor.

The Ink-Jet Printer Made From Lego

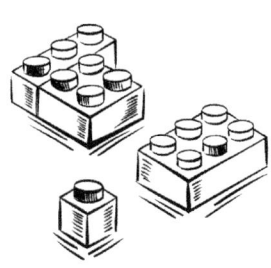

Have you got Lego bricks scattered all over your room—perhaps your living room, where your mom keeps stepping on them and giving you death stares? Well, Larry loved Lego too, but he took those bricks to a whole new level. At the University of Michigan, Larry went on to invent an ink-jet printer with Lego blocks.

He used the blocks to make a line plotter, which is a part of the printer that creates the images or text you want to print. The Lego brick line plotter helped create bigger prints like the ones needed for posters.

He rewired the printer around the Lego structure, so the printer cartridges worked with the Lego brick line plotter. It all sounds fancy and way out, right? But the genius mind of Larry Page was able to figure this out. If you go online and search for 'Images of the Lego Printer Built by Larry Page,' you will get a fair idea of what the printer looked like and how it works.

Page Was on the Solar Car Team

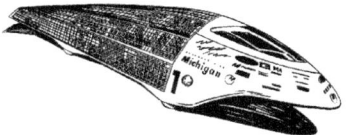

Alright, kids, here's another cool story about Larry Page and a super fun project he was a part of—the Maize and Blue solar car!

When Larry was still at the University of Michigan, he got involved in an exciting team project to build a solar-powered car. This car was called the Maize and Blue, named after the school's colors (Young, 2021)!

The idea was to create a vehicle that could run on sunlight instead of regular fuel. How awesome is that? The team worked hard to design and build the car using special technology and materials to make it lightweight and efficient. Larry used his coding skills and creativity to help as the car was designed to run on software, setting the groundwork for advances in tech in future cars (1993, n.d.).

Not only did the team get to show off their cool solar car, but they also learned a lot about how solar energy works and how it can be used to power vehicles. But here's the best part: This solar car entered a popular solar car race in 1993, called the SunRayce USA, and guess what? The Maize and Blue car won the race (1993, n.d.)!

So, Larry's involvement in the Maize and Blue solar car shows how he was already thinking about big ideas way before he became the awesome co-founder of Google!

On to Stanford University and More Innovations

At Stanford, Larry earned a PhD in Computer Science, where he had a mentor, one of his supervisors, who encouraged Larry to explore an idea he had about understanding the World Wide Web and its structure as a theme for his dissertation. It was probably this dissertation that gave him the brainwave for Google because the amazing search engine was founded while Larry was in Standford.

What Is a Dissertation?

A college dissertation is a super big and important school project that students do when they are finishing their advanced studies, usually for a Master's or a Ph.D. It's their chance to show everything they've learned!

Here's how it works:

1. **Picking a Topic:** First, students choose a topic that interests them—like a big question they want to answer or a problem they want to solve. It could be anything from how plants grow to the effects of video games on kids.

2. **Doing Research:** Next, they spend a lot of time researching. This means looking up books, articles, and studies to gather information about their topic. It's like being a detective, digging up clues and facts!

3. **Writing It Down and Creating an Outline:** After gathering all the information, they create an outline which is like a draft of what the final paper will contain. The draft will have points that they want to discuss and sub-points related to them for in-depth analysis of the subject.

---

4. **Creating the Dissertation:** Once the outline is complete, they use it as a guide to flesh out the points, thereby writing the final draft. They write it out in a big report called a dissertation. This report includes a lot of details about their research, what they discovered, and what they think about it. Think of it like writing a really long essay!

5. **Defending It:** Once they finish, students usually have to stand in front of a group of teachers or experts and explain their work. They answer questions and defend their ideas, kind of like being a superhero standing up for their mission!

In short, a college dissertation is a huge research project where students dive deep into a topic, explore it, and share their findings with others. It's a big step in finishing their college journey and moving into the real world!

Creating Google

Larry Page and his buddy Sergey Brin were studying for their PhDs at Stanford University when they had a brilliant idea! They were working on a project called BackRub; it was all about how websites on the internet are connected. Just like how friends share cool information and links to good stuff, websites do the same thing by linking to one another.

Larry and Sergey noticed that some web pages were linked to lots of other pages, while others were not. They thought, "What if we could use these links to figure out which web pages are the best?" So, they came up with an idea! They created a search engine that would look at these links and see which pages were the most popular and important. The more links a page had from trustworthy sites, the higher it would show up when people searched for something.

This idea became the basis for Google!

They decided that their search engine should show web pages based on how popular they were because they figured that the more popular a page was, the more useful it probably was for people. So, they named their new search engine "Google." Ah and now we get on to the part of how they came up with the odd name—do you know why?

The name comes from the word "googol," which is a huge number—one followed by 100 zeros! Yes, it's super huge. To be more mathematical, it's 10 raised to a power of 100. Can you do the sum?

Would you like to have a googol of different flavored ice creams?

Larry and Sergey worked hard to make their search engine smart, adding tons of information from the web to ensure it gave accurate results. Soon, they needed some money to grow their idea, so they raised $1 million from their family, friends, and other people who believed in them (Vedantu, 2021). I bet Larry's family were huge supporters as they believed in and encouraged Larry to reach his full potential.

In 1998, they launched Google, and it took off like a rocket! Later, in 2004, Google had a big moment when Larry and Sergey allowed other investors to buy a part of their company, in an act called Initial Public Offering (IPO) the move made making Larry and Sergey billionaires! Or is it googolaires!

What Is an IPO?

An IPO, or Initial Public Offering, is like a big event when a private company decides to sell pieces of itself to the public for the first time. Imagine if your favorite toy company wanted to grow and make even more toys, but they needed extra money to do it. So, they invite people to buy shares, which are small parts of the company.

When people buy shares, they become part owners of the company. This helps the company get money to create new toys or expand its business. Plus, once the company goes public, its shares can be bought and sold on the stock market, kind of like trading cards, but for companies! This way, anyone can invest in that company and share in its success.

By 2013, Google became the most popular search engine in the world, with about 5.9 billion searches every day! Wow! Their amazing headquarters is located in California's Silicon Valley, where a lot of the tech magic happens (Sitecentre, 2021)

And that's how Google was formed—a story of friendship, creativity, and the desire to help people find the information they need on the internet. How inspiring is that?

Well, kids, do you agree that Larry and Sergey proved that even small projects can make a big impact if you are passionate and keep trying? Teamwork and a constant need to innovate can help you come up with some brilliant ideas!

Workbook Activity 6: Creating a Fun Dissertation

Imagine you are in college and choose a fun, informal subject you want to explore and write your dissertation about it. Follow the steps given on how a dissertation is formed to gather your information. Use AI and—Google, of course—to gather your information and sort it into an easy-to-understand structure.

Here are some fun sample topics you can use, or even better, come up with your own:

- **Why Cats Are Secretly Aliens in Disguise:** Investigate the funny behaviors of cats and why they might be extraterrestrial beings observing us!

- **The Science of Ice Cream—Why It Melts Faster on Hot Days:** A serious look at the delicious world of ice cream, with some funny anecdotes about how many scoops are too many!

- **Do Superheroes Get Tired?** Explore the idea that superheroes work hard but might just want a nap instead of saving the day all the time!

- **The Great Debate: Are Unicorns Better Than Dinosaurs?** Dive into a playful battle, comparing the magical qualities of unicorns with the amazing features of dinosaurs!

- **Why Do Parents Say "No" to Everything?** A humorous examination of common things kids want to do and the funny reasons parents might give for saying no.

- **The Mystery of Why Socks Disappear in the Laundry:** Investigate where all those missing socks go and propose some hilarious theories about sock thieves!

- **Do Plants Really Like Music?** Experiment with your houseplants to see if they grow better when you sing or play music for them.

- **The History of Whoopee Cushions and Their Impact on Comedy:** Explore the funny world of prank gadgets and how they've made people laugh for generations!

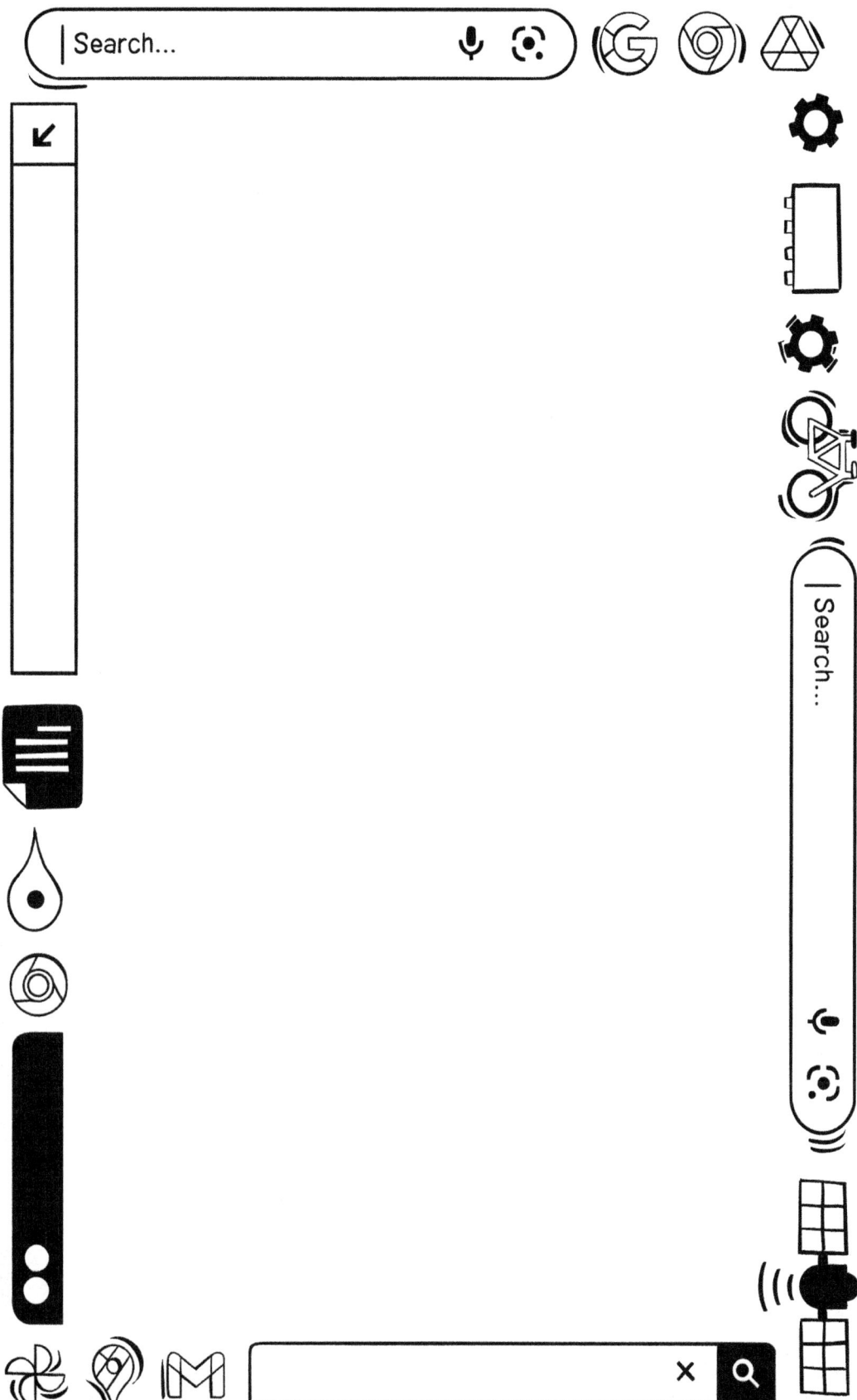

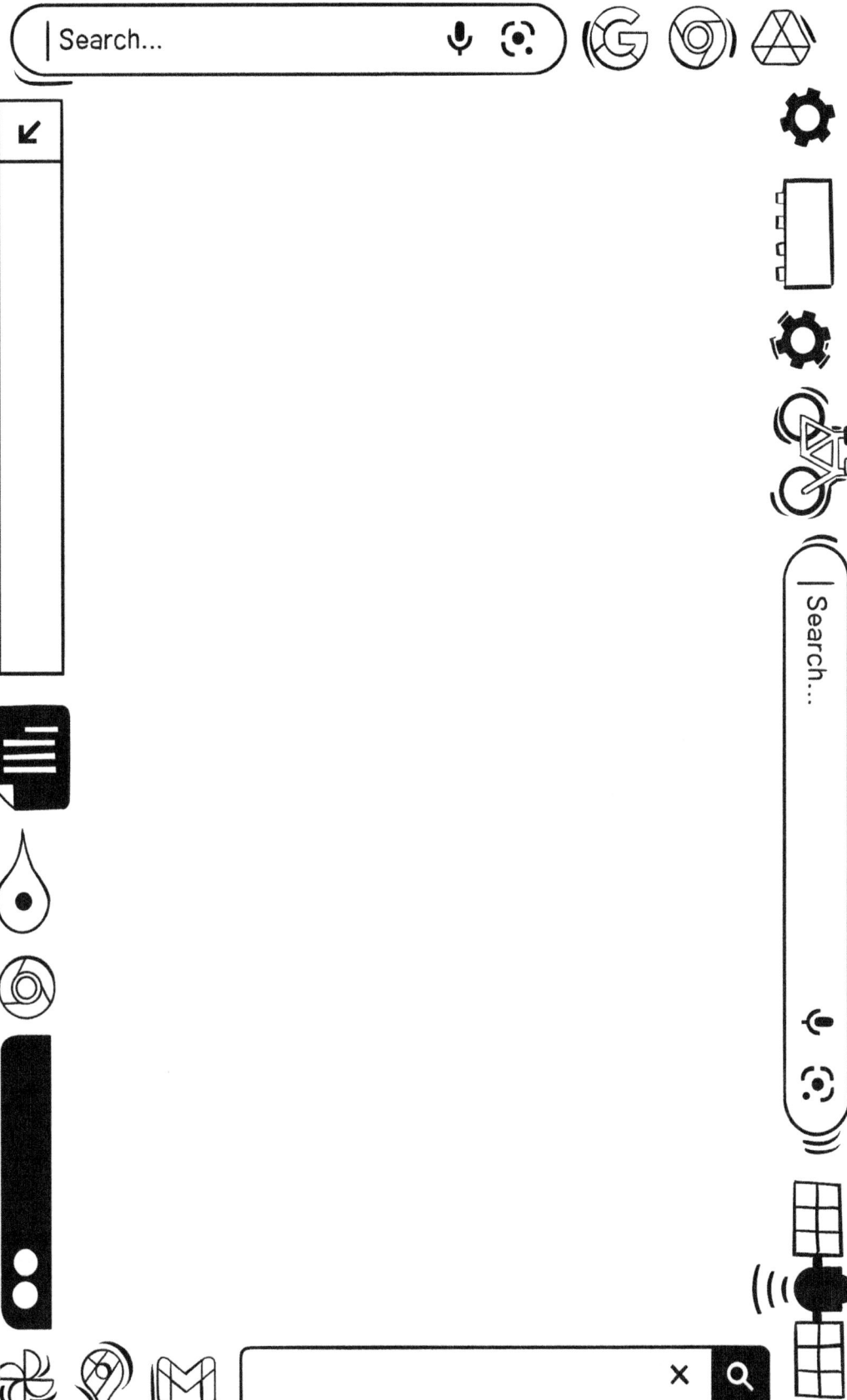

CHAPTER
THIRTEEN
HOW TO BE A TECH TITAN:
YOUR ULTIMATE GUIDE TO BECOMING A FUTURE GENIUS!

Hey there, future innovators and world-changers! Are you ready to embark on an epic adventure toward becoming a tech titan? Well then, buckle up because this is your game plan to navigate the exciting world of awesomeness, filled with education, creativity, and loads of giggles.

Key Traits and Goals for Future Geniuses

Would you like to be a rocket man and help Elon Musk build his Mars colony? Or maybe you want to invent an app like Alibaba to sell awesome candy to kids across the world? Well, if you have dreams, you must have goals, so here are some tips on how to start: "Mission Awesome Inventor!"

Hit the Books Like a Boss

First things first: think of education as your golden ticket to Awesometown! You want to dive into subjects like math and science, which are the secret ingredients for cooking up some serious tech magic.

Imagine yourself as a wizard, with math as your magic potion and science as the shiny dust that makes everything come alive! Let's not forget computer science—your magical wand! With it, you can create cool apps, mind-blowing games, or even a virtual pet that gives you compliments (who wouldn't want that?!).

Those math equations you dread? They're formulas that will help you build virtual worlds or design amazing apps. Science experiments might feel chaotic now, but one day, you might be experimenting with rocket fuel or coding artificial intelligence—thank the science fair for getting you started!

☀ **Action Tip:** Treat your studies like an epic video game quest! Level up in subjects you love, join clubs like coding or robotics, or rock that science fair project that makes everyone go, "Wow!" Embrace every challenge you face as stepping stones to achieving your dreams.

Remember, every great scientist or engineer was just a kid playing in a sandbox of knowledge at one point!

Get Curious—Like a Cat With a Laser Pointer

Curiosity isn't just for cats chasing laser pointers—don't you just love those videos?

Curiosity is your superpower too! The tech titans in our book had an insatiable desire to know how everything worked. Do you wonder what's inside your TV remote? Or why does your granddad's old radio make that funny static sound?

Embrace that detective spirit! Explore, tinker, and ask a million questions. If you don't have adults or mentors to ask questions, get online and search for answers; ask AI, and you are bound to get a comprehensive reply to your question. Your curiosity can unlock doors to amazing discoveries and maybe even lead to the next groundbreaking invention.

You might find that wanting to open up your old gadgets isn't just silly; it's your brain telling you to explore how things function! Being curious leads to exploration. So, don't be shy! Ask questions, dig deeper, and turn your "Why is that?" into "Wow, look what I found!" Just don't take apart your mom's favorite appliances without permission.

Action Tip: Look for a space you can turn into a mini science lab; your room, if you are not sharing it, or any other corner of the house you can use will do—and if you've got one, a corner in the garage.

Ask your parents or any other adult for some tools and start tinkering with gadgets—you get permission to disassemble them. Try to figure out why that squeaky toy makes weird noises, or what makes that little electric engine run. You get bonus points if you can fix it!

Pursue Hobbies as if You're on a Treasure Hunt

Hobbies should feel as exciting as scavenging for hidden treasure! Think about what makes your heart race—whether you're building epic LEGO castles, discovering new worlds in video games, or whipping up computer programs, dive in headfirst! Many tech legends started by exploring their interests and having fun.

Remember how you felt the first time you built something on your own? That's what passion feels like! When you engage in your hobbies, you're not just passing time; you're setting the stage for your future innovations. Remember how Michael Dell made money trading stamps at the age of 12?

🧠 **Action Tip:** Seek out new adventures! Try out clubs, whether it's a robotics team or an art class where you can unleash your creative side, start a YouTube channel where you share your favorite game strategies, or even review the coolest tech toys. Who knows? You might just become the next big YouTube sensation! Try to set a goal where you learn a new talent every year.

Laugh in the Face of Difficulties and Failure

Every tech titan has faced epic fails that made them want to shout, "Why, oh why?!" But here's the twist—they learned from those embarrassing bloopers! Just like Elon Musk and Larry Ellison, when things go wrong, you can turn that spilled paint or twisted science project into a priceless lesson. Even Albert Einstein didn't ace everything right away, you know!

Embracing failure means thinking, "Okay, that didn't work out—what's the next move?" This mindset is what separates a budding inventor from a future superstar. We all trip and fall sometimes, face difficulties, and feel like failures, but what matters is how quickly you get back up and keep trying!

🧠 **Action Tip:** Keep a "Fail Diary" where you jot down your epic fails and what you learned. You can write or doodle about your mistakes. Laughter is the best medicine! When you laugh at your mistakes, they become less scary and way more fun to share.

Build Your Crew—Like the Avengers

You need an awesome squad by your side to help you along your inventor path! Just like superheroes don't fight alone, the great

tech legends had their supporters. Find friends, mentors, and family members who believe in you and cheer you on!

Are you the kind of person who loves talking about cool ideas or testing out new inventions? Surround yourself with friends who are good listeners, and in turn, be one yourself.

Action Tip: Join clubs, online forums, or video game groups that have been approved by your parents or any other adults taking care of you. Remember, it's important for kids to stay safe when they are surfing the web; never give out personal information or visit sites you are not familiar with. Your best mode of action is to ask an adult to help you find suitable sites to connect with fellow creators. With a good crew, you can bounce ideas off while sharing snacks during brainstorming sessions. Because let's be honest—brainpower is fueled by delicious snacks, right?

Become a Lifelong Learner (AKA a Knowledge Ninja)

In our fast-changing tech world, keeping your brain updated is. Treat your mind like your favorite gaming console—always in need of upgrades in the form of information! Jump onto online courses, dive into crazy facts, or read cool tech books.

Dedicating your time to learning helps you become a "Knowledge Ninja"—swift and smart! It will help keep your skills sharp, even improve them, and you'll always be ready to tackle any challenge that comes your way.

Action Tip: Set a fun challenge! Try to read a certain number of books each month about tech legends, inventors, or any topic that interests you—reading takes you to magical realms and a whole new world of discovery. If your parents catch you hoarding books like a dragon with treasure, assure them you're just immersing yourself in new worlds.

Flash That Positive Attitude Like a Superpower

Last but not least, your attitude can be your strongest weapon! Think of it this way: tech titans don't give up; they keep their eyes on the prize. Think of Jensen Huang and all that bullying he endured. Stay upbeat and kick negativity to the curb. Don't forget to share your wacky ideas and dreams with family and friends—who knows? You might just inspire the next big thing! Every inventor started somewhere, right? You have the power to overcome any challenge with a smile and a sprinkle of positivity.

Action Tip: Create fun "I can do it!" statements to hang on your wall. Turn them into colorful posters or doodles that make you smile whenever you walk by. They'll serve as your personal cheerleaders, reminding you that you've got this!

Here are some samples:

1. "Believe in yourself! You have the power to make amazing things happen!"

2. "Every great success starts with the words 'I can do it!' So go ahead and shine!"

3. "When things get tough, just remember: you're strong enough to keep going!"

4. "Dream big and say 'I can do it!' because you are unstoppable!"

5. "Give it your best shot! There's nothing you can't achieve if you believe!"

Are you ready to embark on this fantastic adventure? With your curiosity ignited, hobbies explored, and a supportive crew alongside you, you're on your way to realizing your dreams. Embrace your uniqueness, stay curious, and remember—every great achievement begins with a dream waiting to take flight! Let the adventure begin! Go forth and innovate, young dreamers!

Study Paths for Future Entrepreneurs and Tech Titan

Here is a breakdown of study paths you must follow to achieve your dreams of being a tech titan or entrepreneur

College Prep for Future Entrepreneurs and Tech Titans

If you want to become an entrepreneur (someone who starts their own business) or a tech titan (a leader in technology), here's how to get ready for college and beyond!

Becoming an Entrepreneur

1. **Business Studies**
   - **Why It's Important:** Learning about how businesses work is super important. It helps you understand how to market your products, manage money, and organize your company.
   - **What to Study:** Look for classes in business education, entrepreneurship, and economics during high school. These will give you the basic tools to start your own business one day!

2. **Mathematics**
   - **Why It's Important:** Math skills are key for handling budgets and making smart financial decisions. You'll need to calculate profits and expenses, and analyze data.
   - **What to Study:** Focus on algebra and statistics. These subjects will help you make informed choices in your business ventures later on.

3. **Communication Skills**
   - **Why It's Important:** Being able to clearly express your ideas and negotiate with others is a good habit to foster. Good communication helps you build strong relationships.
   - **What to Study:** Take courses in English, public speaking, and debate. These classes will improve your speaking and writing skills, which are important when pitching ideas.

4. **Creative Thinking**
   - **Why It's Important:** Creativity is what leads to new ideas and solutions. Thinking outside the box can help you stand out in a crowded market.
   - **What to Study:** Get involved in art, theater, or creative writing classes. They will help you enhance your brainstorming abilities and develop innovative concepts.

5. **Leadership and Teamwork**
   - **Why It's Important:** Entrepreneurs often work with a team, and good leadership helps you guide others effectively.
   - **What to Study:** Join group projects and participate in leadership clubs or sports teams. These experiences will teach you how to collaborate and lead with confidence.

Becoming a Tech Titan

If you want to make a difference in the tech world, here are additional subjects to focus on:

1. **Computer Science**
   - **Why It's Important:** Learning about programming and software development is essential for anyone aiming to lead in technology.
   - **What to Study:** Take courses in computer programming, web development, and information technology. These subjects provide the foundation for understanding coding and software.

2. **Engineering**
   - **Why It's Important:** Engineering teaches you problem-solving skills and gives you a solid understanding of how technology operates.
   - **What to Study:** Look for classes in electrical, mechanical, or software engineering. They will prepare you for various tech-related careers.

3. **Data Analysis**
   - **Why It's Important:** Making decisions based on data is important in technology. Knowing how to analyze and interpret data can give you a competitive advantage.
   - **What to Study:** Classes in data science, statistics, and math are important for learning how to work with data effectively.

4. **Entrepreneurial Mindset**
   - **Why It's Important:** Being open to innovation and willing to take risks is key in the tech industry. This mindset helps you thrive in fast-changing environments.
   - **What to Study:** Work on projects that challenge you and encourage creativity. Learning to solve problems in new ways will help you succeed as a tech titan.

College Prep

Whether you're aiming to become an entrepreneur or a tech titan, you must start with the right subjects and a passion for learning. Dive into your studies, embrace challenges, and nurture your curiosity. Who knows? You could be the next great innovator to change the world!

Getting prepared for college is all about selecting the right subjects and gaining hands-on experiences that can set you up for future success. Embrace every chance to learn, ask questions, and explore your interests. With hard work, passion, and the right knowledge, you could become the next big entrepreneur or tech innovator! Keep reaching for your dreams!

Are You Ready to Shine?

So there you have it, future inventors! You're armed with tools, tricks, and tons of inspiration to tackle your dreams like a superhero taking on a supervillain. Remember to keep asking, "How does this work?" and "Can I make it cooler?" Keep that wonder alive!

Don't just skate through school; treat your studies like an epic quest— complete with wacky side adventures and maybe even a secret lair! You might one day be the person who invents the next must-have gadget or the game that everyone wants to play. Just remember: your imagination is limitless, and the world is your playground. Go out there and make your mark! And always keep a snack handy for those brainstorming sessions—after all, great ideas need fuel! Let the innovation begin!

CHAPTER

FOURTEEN
NURTURING FUTURE INNOVATORS

Dear Parents,

You hold the incredible power to shape your child's future because the seeds of creativity, curiosity, and resilience you nurture today will blossom into the traits that lead them to success in the future.

Think of the many tech titans we admired in this book; most had one thing in common: unwavering support from their parents. This guidance played an important role in helping them overcome challenges and reach their full potential.

Many of these innovators didn't come from privileged backgrounds. For instance, consider Jensen Huang, who faced daunting circumstances when he moved to a new country. His childhood was filled with obstacles, but the arrival of his supportive parents marked a turning point in his life as a signal for his genius to thrive. Together, they built a foundation of resilience that allowed him to become the success he is today.

Even the smallest acts of encouragement can motivate your child in meaningful ways. Take Larry Ellison, for example. Despite a tumultuous relationship with his adoptive father, it was his adoptive mother's encouragement that kept him on track. She helped him discover his true potential, guiding him away from negativity and toward amazing achievements. Larry could have chosen the wrong path, given the hurt, anger, and disappointment that would have been a part of his childhood, but that one supportive figure in his life was enough to keep him grounded.

Remember Jack Ma, whose parents, while not technologically savvy or wealthy, prioritized education and encouraged their son through his struggles and setbacks. Their steadfast belief in him paved the way for Jack to overcome challenges and ultimately achieve his teaching credentials, opening doors to endless opportunities.

As you nurture your little one, remember that every word of encouragement you offer is a valuable investment in their transition from childhood to innovator. Your support, patience, and passionate guidance make a huge difference.

However, parents need to find a balance between encouragement and overindulgence. Too much support without healthy boundaries can lead to a child becoming entitled and emotionally fragile, which could hinder their future success. It can be challenging to strike that balance, but with thoughtful parenting, you can help them grow into resilient individuals who are prepared to face the world.

You are sowing the seeds of greatness in them, equipping them to confront challenges with curiosity, courage, and the confidence to pursue their dreams. Together, let's cultivate an environment where they can explore, learn, and thrive!

Embracing Uniqueness: Crafting a Personalized Path to Success for Your Child

Every child is unique, displaying different characteristics, talents, and needs. Your role as a parent is to understand what's special about your child or children and nurture their abilities, curiosity, and aspirations. By tailoring your support to fit their individual qualities, you're crafting a personalized formula for success.

The Role of Parents in Nurturing Creativity and Innovation

You serve as a pivotal figure in shaping your child's creativity, curiosity, and resilience to failure. You can create a foundation for your kid to explore the world around them. For example, Elon Musk's mother encouraged his inquisitive nature, which allowed him to explore different interests from an early age.

As a parent, you can encourage this kind of environment by providing opportunities for hands-on learning. This means allowing your child—or children—to experiment with different activities, which can be as simple as building with blocks or trying out different art supplies. Such activities provide a space for your child to make mistakes without fear. This approach nurtures creativity and boosts problem-solving skills. When your child engages in open-ended tasks, they will learn to think critically, becoming innovative as they seek solutions to the difficulties they might face.

Encouraging your child to explore art, music, or any other creative hobby is important for their emotional well-being. These activities provide a healthy outlet for self-expression, allowing them to process feelings and manage stress. When the pressures of modern childhood become overwhelming, engaging in creative pursuits can help them feel grounded and centered. This feeds their imagination and critical thinking skills, but it also promotes resilience and emotional stability. By supporting their artistic endeavors, you're equipping them with tools to face challenges and positively express themselves, ultimately enhancing their overall happiness and confidence.

Supporting Exploration and Learning

Providing an environment that celebrates exploration can lead to valuable lessons. You can set up science projects at home; they are not that hard; just search using the following phrases: "Easy science projects for kids to do at home."

Encourage or initiate visits to museums, especially science museums with interactive displays kids can explore. If you have a computer-savvy whizz at home, let your child try their hand at coding. Yes, coding can be mastered by children as young as 5 or 7... remember Larry Page! By doing such things, you can guide your child to keep asking questions and seeking answers.

Setting aside regular time for exploration allows your child to dive deep into subjects that interest them. Perhaps they are curious about how things work, prompting them to take apart an old toy and reassemble it. So go on and get them some cheap electronic gadgets that are safe to disassemble and enjoy your child's enthusiasm. Each exploration helps them develop skills and confidence that will serve them in the future.

Importance of Parental Support During Challenges

In addition to encouraging creativity, your support for your child in the face of adversity is vital. Many successful figures, such as Steve Jobs and Jeff Bezos, attribute their achievements to supportive families who recognize their unique interests. For instance, Jobs' parents encouraged his passion for electronics, allowing him to pursue his interests without reservation, even when he decided to drop out of college.

Parents should aim to guide their children. Setting high but realistic expectations allows your child to strive for excellence on their terms, minus the pressure. It is equally important to recognize and celebrate their individuality. Children thrive when they feel their unique qualities are valued, often leading to significant achievements in their lives.

Embrace Your Child's Individual Learning Capacities

Every child learns at their own unique pace, progressing through different phases of development and discovery. Parents must recognize and celebrate these individual accomplishments rather than compare their child's progress to that of others. Comparing can lead to unnecessary pressure and feelings of inadequacy, hindering a child's natural growth and enthusiasm for learning. Instead, parents should focus on encouragement, providing a supportive environment that nurtures their child's interests and abilities. By emphasizing their child's strengths and celebrating milestones, parents can help instill confidence and a love for learning, helping their child thrive in their educational adventure.

Building Resilience and Confidence

Handling challenges is another area where parents play an important role. Take the examples of Elon Musk, Jack Ma, Jensen Huang, and Mark Zuckerberg, all of whom faced bullying during their youth.

You play an important role in helping your child face challenges. By instilling values of perseverance and self-advocacy, you empower them to respond positively to adversity as a curveball that life throws at you, because "hey, these things happen."

Encourage your child to be prepared to face challenges, to seek help when needed, and teach them constructive ways to handle issues. This support builds confidence and resilience, invaluable traits that will serve your child well throughout their lives.

Nurturing a Love for Reading and Lifelong Learning

Nurturing a love for reading and a commitment to continuous learning is needed for children's development and growth. Even if you aren't an avid reader yourself or don't have an extensive library at home, there are many ways to inspire your child's passion for books. Introducing your child to impactful literature can open up new worlds and ideas, enriching their imagination.

You can also find resources online that recommend age-appropriate books your child is likely to enjoy. Consider setting aside regular times for read-aloud sessions, which can ignite your child's curiosity and encourage a love for stories and knowledge. Simply being present while your child completes their homework—offering support and encouragement—can make a significant difference to their learning experience. Remember, your involvement and enthusiasm can help lay the foundation for a lifelong love of reading and learning.

Communication and Value of Diverse Perspectives

Open communication is key to nurturing children's dreams and aspirations. Children are highly intelligent and value being treated as individuals. Engaging in regular discussions about your child's interests allows them to express themselves freely.

Maintain a habit of listening to your child's ideas, validating their thoughts. By doing this, you are helping your child feel encouraged to share more with you and develop a sense of belonging to the family unit.

Celebrating diverse perspectives in your family will enhance collaboration and understanding between parents and also siblings. As a parent, you can introduce your child to different cultures and viewpoints through travel, discussion, and community involvement. Such experiences will broaden your child's horizons and strengthen their capacity to see the world through various lenses.

The Transformative Role of Parents

Overall, you play a transformative role in your child's life. You provide encouragement, build interest, and tell them about the importance of resilience and collaboration.

This blend of support helps your child realize that every great achievement begins with a dream and establishing small goals. It is through both personal effort and your guidance that these dreams can take flight. We live in a busy world where parents are juggling work and family life. They try hard to create a healthy home atmosphere through all of life's challenges, so remember that being involved in your child's life doesn't have to be overwhelming; you are not expected to ace through parenting. We all make mistakes and have shortfalls, but using them as learning curves to help our children is the key to success.

Simple actions like showing up for school events, acknowledging achievements, or being available to talk can make a world of difference. These small but meaningful gestures build strong bonds between children and parents or caregivers and lay the groundwork for a successful future.

Creating an Enriching Environment

Encourage critical thinking; this means asking open-ended questions that provoke thought and discussion. For example, instead of just saying, "What did you learn today?"

You could ask, "What part of your day excited you the most, and why is that?" This approach invites deeper conversation and helps children articulate their feelings and thoughts. The goal is not to create pressure, but to create a space where children feel comfortable to share their insights and questions. If you've got a very talkative kid at home, you know what I mean and how much this type of conversation will be appreciated. Never shut down a child who is enthusiastically talking to you about an important part of their day. Stop what you are doing and give them your time for just two minutes, and you will gain a little buddy who loves, respects, and looks for you in times of trouble.

Guiding Children Through Setbacks

In the face of challenges, such as academic setbacks or friendship issues, you can offer your child constructive advice. Instead of providing quick solutions, you might ask guiding questions that help your child to think through the problem.

For instance, if your child is struggling with a project, instead of doing it for them, you could say, "What do you think is the most challenging part of this project for you?"

This allows your child to rethink their approach to the project, attempting to identify ways to overcome the challenges they are facing. Subtly providing tools for problem-solving in this manner builds emotional intelligence and confidence.

By being an active participant in your child's life, you can contribute significantly to their development. The supportive actions taken at home set the foundation for children to blossom into resilient, curious, and innovative individuals. Encouraging them to pursue their dreams and not shy away from difficulties equips them for future success.

Place Emphasis on Education

Education shapes your child's future and sets the foundation for success and personal development. Many inspiring stories of innovators and leaders highlight the common factor of families who prioritize learning.

For example, Larry Page, co-founder of Google, thrived in a home where education was valued, and curiosity was encouraged. His parents motivated him to ask questions and seek answers, allowing his natural interests to flourish.

By prioritizing education, you convey its importance, inspiring your child to develop a love for learning and pursue knowledge with gusto. This foundation helps them embrace challenges, cultivate a growth mindset, and become resilient problem solvers.

Support Your Gifted Child

Supporting gifted children, in particular, is vital. These children may require additional resources or advanced learning opportunities to keep them engaged. You can support suitable lessons, challenge them with difficult topics, and offer activities that fit their skills. It's important to create an environment that nurtures their talents while also encouraging social and emotional development.

Investing in education enhances your child's academic skills and also boosts their self-esteem. When they experience success, such as achieving good grades or reaching personal milestones, they gain confidence that propels them forward. Ultimately, emphasizing education empowers all children, including gifted individuals, to recognize that learning can open doors to a brighter, more promising future.

Role Models and Mentorship

You, as parents, serve as the first role models in your child's life. By guiding them through struggles and challenges, demonstrating resilience and determination, you are setting a high standard for them.

For example, Dell's parents played a significant role by exhibiting how hard work and perseverance could lead to success. When children see their parents overcoming obstacles, they learn the value of hard work. These experiences teach them that it's okay to face setbacks and that they can get back up and keep moving forward.

Moral Values and Empathy

Lessons in moral values and empathy for children are important. Parents often play an important role in imparting these values. As you teach your child about compassion, humility, and the importance of helping others, you are helping them develop a sense of empathy, setting the foundation for them to embrace moral values that you cherish.

One striking example is Reed Hastings, who started a fund for underprivileged schools. His parents influenced his strong sense of social responsibility, showing him that success should also include a commitment to giving back. When parents impart these values, children learn to be better citizens. They grow up understanding that their actions can make a difference in the lives of others, creating a more empathetic and caring society.

These traits help create innovative thinkers who can achieve great things. This shows that caring and understanding parenting is crucial for children to reach their full potential.

Unless you are already implementing these strategies, by doing so you will create a nurturing environment that lays the groundwork for your child's development into a resilient, curious, and innovative individual.

Your support and involvement can make a significant impact, helping them realize that every great achievement begins with a simple dream. Equip your child with the tools to soar, and watch them embrace greatness!

CONCLUSION:
IGNITING THE SPARK OF POTENTIAL

As we wrap up our adventures across the childhood stories of some of the brightest tech innovators of our time, let's take a moment to reflect on what we've learned. From Elon Musk's boundless curiosity to Steve Jobs' unwavering determination, it's clear that an incredible future can begin from humble beginnings. Each of these innovators faced unique challenges, but their stories remind us that perseverance and hard work can lead to remarkable achievements.

Every dream starts with a bit of imagination. Let the stories of these innovators inspire your own goals. You can create amazing things, overcome challenges, and make a real difference in the world. Use feedback as a helpful tool for growth; it can improve your ideas on your way to success. So, go out there, dream big, and start writing your own story! The future is yours to shape, and we look forward to seeing what you will achieve!

Please Leave Me a Review

I'd love to hear your thoughts! If you enjoyed this book, please leave me a review. Are there more tech titans or other people you'd like us to explore? What other aspects of their lives are you curious about? Your input is really important to me and helps me create content that you want to read.

Stay tuned for more exciting books in this series! Thank you for joining me on this adventure!

REFERENCES

Acharya, P. S. (2025). *10 Rejections From Harvard And 30 Failed Job Interviews: How Jack Ma Became One Of China's Richest Men.* Msn. https://msn./en-us/money/news/10-rejections-from-harvard-and-30-failed-job-interviews-how-jack-ma-became-one-of-china-s-richest-men/ss-AA1pw9jT

Admin. (2022, August 22). *From A Design Teacher To An Entrepreneur: A Billon Dollar Story Of "Canva".* TheAussieway. https://theaussieway.au/from-a-design-teacher-to-an-entrepreneur-a-billon-dollar-story-of-canva/

Alfar, G. (2024, January 15). *What's a great way for kids to grow up? Tidbits from what we know about Elon Musk's childhood.* Whats up tesla. https://whatsuptesla/2024/01/15/whats-a-great-way-for-kids-to-grow-up-tidbits-from-what-we-know-about-elon-musks-childhood/

Apple, V. (2025). *Current Huang fellows.* Duke University Science & society. https://scienceandsociety.duke.edu/learn/undergraduate-programs/huang-fellows-program/profiles-of-huang-fellows/

Beaver, C. (2023a, May 30). Uncovering Reed Hastings' secrets to success. *Advisorycloud.* https://advisorycloud/blog/uncovering-reed-hastings-secrets-to-success

Beaver, C. (2023b, May 30). Uncovering the secrets to Larry Ellison's success. *Advisorycloud.* https://advisorycloud/blog/uncovering-the-secrets-to-larry-ellisons-success

Biography.com Editors. (2020, July 17). *Michael dell - family, computers & facts.* Biography. https://biography/business-leaders/michael-dell

BrandWagon Online. (2024, November 5). *Financial express.* Financial Express. https://financialexpress/business/

brandwagon-dell-laptops-retains-title-of-1-most-desired-brand-reveals-tras-report-3656289/

Candid. (2016, January 14). *Reed Hastings creates $100 million education fund.* Philanthropy News Digest (PND). https://philanthropynewsdigest.org/news/reed-hastings-creates-100-million-education-fund

Cherished forever. (2024). Confinity.com. https://confinity/legacies/steve-jobs

Class notes - graduate studies. (2025). Brownalumnimagazine.com. https://brownalumnimagazine/classes/class-notes-graduate-studies

Danielson, T. (2025, January 6). *How Melanie Perkins and Canva revolutionized the world.* Beta Boom. https://betaboom/melanie-perkins-and-canva-revolutionized-the-world/

Dell Technologies. (2023). *Our timeline.* Dell Technologies US. https://dell/en-us/dt/corporate/about-us/who-we-are/timeline.html

Dennon, A. (2021). *Did Jeff Bezos go to college?* BestColleges.com. https://bestcolleges/news/2021-2/10/29/did-jeff-bezos-go-to-college/

Devlin, H. (2024, August 14). *Scientists find humans age dramatically in two bursts – at 44, then 60.* The Guardian. https://theguardian/science/article/2024/aug/14/scientists-find-humans-age-dramatically-in-two-bursts-at-44-then-60-aging-not-slow-and-steady

Dr. Sajeev Dev. (2024, August 20). *The inspirational journey of jack ma: From rejections to revolutionizing global e-commerce.* Dr. Sajeev Dev. https://sajeevdev/the-inspirational-journey-of-jack-ma-from-rejections-to-revolutionizing-global-e-commerce/

Editor BizNews. (2023, September 12). *Elon Musk's Turbulent South African upbringing: from Bullying to Bloodshed.* BizNews.com. https://biznews/leadership/2023/09/12/elon-musks-turbulent-upbringing

Fabritius, F. (2023, February 7). *A neuroscientist shares the 4 "highly coveted" skills that set introverts apart: "Their brains work differently."* CNBC. https://cnbc/2023/02/07/neuroscientist-shares-coveted-skills-that-set-introverts-apart-their-brains-work-differently.html

Farzan, A. (n.d.). *From a college dropout to a $54 billion fortune — the incredible rags-to-riches story of Oracle founder Larry Ellison*. Business Insider. https://businessinsider/rags-to-riches-story-of-larry-ellison-2015-5

First job Fridays: Reed Hastings. (2016, November 25). Information Station. https://informationstation.org/kitchen_table_econ/first-job-fridays-reed-hastings/

Girdhar, K. (2024, February 2). *Comprehensive guide on stitch-fix business model*. InfoStride. https://infostride/stitch-fix-business-model/

Hall, M. (2024, March 30). *Facebook*. Britannica. https://britannica/money/Facebook

Haroon, R. (2020, June 30). *Why Steve Jobs dropped out of college*. Medium. https://medium/@rumeena36/why-steve-jobs-dropped-the-college-30de0367d0db

How Jeff Bezos Was Raised. (2022, November 14). Clever Tykes. https://clevertykes/how-jeff-bezos-was-raised/

Huddleston Jr, T. (2024). *Jeff Bezos valedictorian speech*. Google. https://google/search?client=safari&rls=en&q=jeff+bezos+valedictorian+speech&ie=UTF-8&oe=UTF-8

Ian. (2024, December 6). *Jack Ma's childhood and personal life before Alibaba*. Pressfarm. https://press.farm/jack-mas-childhood-and-life-before-alibaba/

Isaacson, W. (2012, September 1). *How Steve Jobs' love of simplicity fueled A design revolution*. Smithsonian. https://smithsonianmag/arts-culture/how-steve-jobs-love-of-simplicity-fueled-a-design-revolution-23868877/

Jain, S. (2024, July 21). The Netflix revolution - part 1: History of Netflix. *VdoCipher Blog*. https://vdocipher/blog/2017/06/netflix-revolution-part-1-history/

Jensen Huang. (2024). Fasterthannormal.co. https://fasterthannormal.co/people/jensen-huang

Jess. (2024, March 3). *Melanie Perkins - revolutionising design through entrepreneurial vision*. Inspirepreneur. https://inspirepreneurmagazine/melanie-perkins-revolutionising-design-through-entrepreneurial-vision/

Jobs, S. (2024, November 22). *Our mental health.* Our Mental Health. https://ourmental.health/celebtypes/decoding-steve-jobs-the-personality-behind-the-tech-visionary

Johnson, E. (2019, July 24). *In 10 years, every "relevant" company will be a tech company, Stitch Fix CEO Katrina Lake says.* Vox. https://vox/recode/2019/7/24/20707751/katrina-lake-stitch-fix-retail-fashion-clothing-data-kara-swisher-recode-decode-podcast-interview

Karmali, N. (2024). Australia's 50 richest 2024. *Forbes.* https://forbes/lists/australia-billionaires/

Katrina Lake | bof 500 | the people shaping the global fashion industry. (2020, June 28). The Business of Fashion. https://businessoffashion/people/katrina-lake/

Katrina Lake. (2022, May 2). Gold House. https://goldhouse.org/people/katrina-lake-4/

Khan, N. (n.d.). *Elon Musk biography - early life, qualification, works and success story.* VEDANTU. https://vedantu/biography/elon-musk#

King, L. (2020, March 22). *Who said creativity is intelligence having fun?* Medium. https://medium/mindset-matters/who-said-creativity-is-intelligence-having-fun-f5cae35f5c1d

Larry Page biography. (2021, August 10). Vedantu. https://vedantu/biography/larry-page

Larry Page. (2022, March 4). Academy of Achievement. https://achievement.org/achiever/larry-page/

Loser, R. (2023). *Jensen Huang's life and company – NVIDIA: Building supercomputers today for tomorrow's AI, his prediction of AGI by 2028 and his thoughts on AI safety, prosperity and new jobs.* JD Supra. https://jdsupra/legalnews/jensen-huang-s-life-and-company-nvidia-7241153/

M, I. (2024, October 21). *What was Jeff Bezos like as a child? His formative years.* AdviceScout. https://advicescout/what-was-jeff-bezos-like-as-a-child/?srsltid=AfmBOorM2ubDc30CL-ly91pjpEW-dMsmrUWUzy6bpHh19DAUc6TVUWKs

Ma, J. (2018). *Jack Ma | success stories.* Novpad. https://novpad/en/read/486/7177

Mark Zuckerberg - facebook, family & facts. (2019, October 24). Biography. https://biography/business-leaders/mark-zuckerberg

Michael S Dell. (2008, October 9). Academy of Achievement. https://entrepreneur/growing-a-business/michael-dell/197566

Norris, J. (n.d.). *The volunteer who became the co-founder and CEO of Netflix— Reed Hastings (Swaziland) – Peace Corps Worldwide*. Peacecorpsworldwide. org. https://peacecorpsworldwide.org/the-volunteer-who-became-the-co-founder-and-ceo-of-netflixa-profile-in-citizenship-reed-hastings-swaziland/

NVIDIA. (2019). *Self-Driving cars technology & solutions from NVIDIA automotive*. NVIDIA. https://nvidia/en-us/self-driving-cars/

1993 Maize & Blue. (n.d.). University of Michigan Solar Car Team. https://solarcar.engin.umich.edu/1993

Okemwa, K. (2024, February 28). *NVIDIA CEO says the future of coding as a career might already be dead in the water with the imminent prevalence of AI*. Yahoo Tech. https://yahoo/tech/nvidia-ceo-says-future-coding-124534339.html

Paul Jobs. (n.d.). All about steve jobs.com. https://allaboutstevejobs/bio/key_people/paul_jobs

Piccotti, T. (2023, May 22). *Steve Jobs: Apple cofounder and tech innovator*. Biography. https://biography/business-leaders/steve-jobs#steve-jobs-parents-and-adoption

Piccotti, T., & Carusso, C. (2022, October 31). *Elon Musk - Tesla, Age & Family*. Biography. https://biography/business-leaders/elon-musk#

Prequel Community. (2023). *Steve Jobs' wisdom: 5 career lessons to teach your child*. Prequel. https://newsletter.joinprequel/p/steve-jobs-career-lessons-for-kids

Press, G. (2018, April 8). Why Facebook triumphed over all other social networks. *Forbes*. https://forbes/sites/gilpress/2018/04/08/why-facebook-triumphed-over-all-other-social-networks/

Ramanathan, T. (2024, March 21). *Britannica money*. Britannica. https://britannica.com/money/Larry-Page

Rudulph, H. W. (2016, May 31). *Get that life: How I founded an online personal shopping company.* Cosmopolitan. https://cosmopolitan/career/a59033/katrina-lake-stitch-fix-get-that-life/

Sharma, A. (2024, September 15). *8 exceptional books loved and recommended by elon musk.* Times of India. https://timesofindia.indiatimes/life-style/books/web-stories/8-exceptional-books-loved-and-recommended-by-elon-musk/photostory/113362200.cms#

SIR. (2024, September 5). *The Reed Hastings' story: The GOAT who founded Netflix.* Medium. https://medium/@barronqasem/the-reed-hastings-story-the-goat-who-founded-netflix-8acfe294d0af

Srinivasan, H. (2024). *Jeff Bezos' net worth is 12 figures—how he grew his empire from garage startup to global giant.* Investopedia. https://investopedia/jeff-bezos-net-worth-8741170

Steve Jobs and Steve Wozniak. (2023). Lemelson-MIT. https://lemelson.mit.edu/resources/steve-jobs-and-steve-wozniak

Stone, M. (2014, July 10). *Life of Michael Dell.* Business Insider. https://businessinsider/life-of-michael-dell-2014-7#when-he-was-in-high-school-he-got-a-job-selling-newspaper-subscriptions-after-figuring-out-how-to-target-an-untapped-customer-base-he-made-18000-in-just-one-year-2

16 historic figures and celebrities who have dyslexia. (2019, December 18). Touch-Type Read and Spell (TTRS). https://readandspell/famous-people-with-dyslexia

The Academic Paper That Started Google. (2019, October 28). *Cornell University.* https://blogs.cornell.edu/info2040/2019/10/28/the-academic-paper-that-started-google/

The history of Google search — 1998 to 2023+. (2021, July 16). Sitecentre®. https://sitecentre.au/blog/history-of-google-search

Tucker, J. (2023, May 10). *Michael Dell: Computer revolution.* Headspace. https://headspacegroup.co.uk/michael-dell-computer-revolution/

Tykes, C. (2022, March 4). *Mark Zuckerberg's childhood, parents and upbringing.* Clever Tykes. https://clevertykes/mark-zuckerbergs-middle-school-invention/

Van, B. (2016, March). *4 startups Mark Zuckerberg created before Facebook*. BunlongVan. http://geekhmer.github.io/blog/2016/03/01/4-startups-mark-zuckerberg-created-before-facebook/

Volle, A. (2024). *Britannica money*. Britannica.com. https://britannica/money/Jensen-Huang

Wagner, K. (2017, May 23). *Before Facebook, Mark Zuckerberg built a chat network called Zucknet*. Vox. https://vox/2017/5/23/15683074/facebook-mark-zuckerberg-chat-network-aol-zucknet

Ward, M. (2017, May 15). *The no. 1 advantage Mark Zuckerberg and other introverts have over extroverts*. CNBC. https://cnbc/2017/05/15/mark-zuckerberg-and-other-introverts-have-an-advantage-over-extroverts.html

When They Were Young. (2021, June 13). *Young larry page*. Medium. https://youngstars.medium/young-larry-page-4f69eba3002c

Winford, B. (2024, February 20). *The remarkable story of Melanie Perkins - from idea to icon*. Thriday. https://thriday.au/blog-posts/the-remarkable-story-of-melanie-perkins-from-idea-to-icon

Witt, S. (2023, November 27). *How Jensen Huang's Nvidia is powering the A.I. revolution*. The New Yorker. https://newyorker/magazine/2023/12/04/how-jensen-huangs-nvidia-is-powering-the-ai-revolution

Yazdinian, N. G. (2024, September 27). *Steve Jobs and Steve Wozniak's first project Blue Box!* Medium. https://medium/@nyelizabeth/steve-jobs-and-steve-wozniak-first-project-blue-box-a46d6b0d8d51#:~:text=Steve%20Jobs%20and%20Steve%20Wozniak%20created%20a%20blue%20box%20that,of%20infrastructure%20in%20the%20world.

Printed in Dunstable, United Kingdom